How To **Custom Paint Your Car**

How To **Custom Paint Your Car**

JoAnn Bortles of *Crazy Horse Painting*

MOTORBOOKS

Dedication

To Alyre Surette—Artist, craftsman, father, husband, friend, extraordinary card player. Mr. Surette was a great inspiration to me growing up. His workshop was always neat and organized. I never heard him raise his voice. The incredible sheetmetal fabrications he created ran from huge installations in the World Trade Center to pristine art deco lamps. His creations were inspired and original. Always a gentleman.

First published in 2006 by Motorbooks, an imprint of MBI Publishing Company, Galtier Plaza, Suite 200, 380 Jackson Street, St. Paul, MN 55101-3885 USA

Copyright © 2006 by JoAnn Bortles

MBI Publishing Company titles are also available at discounts in bulk quantity for industrial or sales-promotional use. For details write to Special Sales Manager at MBI Publishing Company, Galtier Plaza, Suite 200, 380 Jackson Street, St. Paul, MN 55101-3885 USA

ISBN-13: 978-0-7603-2311-3
ISBN-10: 0-7603-2311-9

On the cover: Realistic flame painting requires careful attention to detail. Notice the small licks of flame trailing off the wheel well.

Inset: Pinup girls are classic custom paint subjects dating back to the classic days of hot rodding.

On the back cover: Skulls can give your car a wicked attitude. In this technique, stencils are used for the shape of the bones and colors are carefully matched.

About the author

JoAnn Bortles owns Crazy Horse Painting in Waxhaw, North Carolina, a top custom paint shop used by many of today's best builders. Her paint work has graced cover bikes on all of the major chopper magazines, including *Easyriders* and *American Iron*. An accomplished writer and photographer, JoAnn's articles have appeared in *The Horse* magazine.

Editor: Peter Schletty
Designer: Chris Fayers

Printed in China

CONTENTS

ACKNOWLEDGMENTS

Thanks to Ryan Young and Ben Jordan. They helped out big time on making some of the projects in this book actually happen.

Big thank you to DanAm SATAusa. Their spray equipment makes my life easier and they are wonderful people. Jim Bortles, my husband, thanks for putting up with me.

And more thanks to: Skip Chance, Shelley Cullen and Chris Hughes of House of Kolor; Click Baldwin of Carolina Harley Davidson; Jon Kosmoski; Knut and Bent Jorganson; Tony Larimer; Mike Lavelle; Gary Glass of Iwata Media; Dave Nichols; Aaron Stevenson; Raymond Mayes; Jerry Pigg; Dr. George Pinsak; Rick Woodin; Darwin Holmstrom; Lindsey Beattie; Sara Liberte; Wayne Springs; Kevin O' Malley; Sheri Tashjian Vega; Ginny Ross Jefferies; Morgan Storm; Goth Girl.

And very special thanks to MaryAnn Surette Beattie

FOREWORD

As you must have been thinking when you picked up this book, the ultimate touch to any prized automobile is the mint condition of its bodywork and paint. Whether you're about to restore a classic or build the ultimate hot rod or just want to impress the locals at cruise night, a knowledge of the techniques of professional painting can mean the difference between an OK job and a showstopper.

This is what JoAnn brings to this book: Countless helpful tips for expert body repair, refinishing, and custom works of art. With the high cost of labor today, a book like this is especially welcome to the do-it-yourselfer. Based upon my personal experience in the hot rod world and, most recently, the custom motorcycle world, this book offers priceless information on the tricks of the trade from pounding out, to welding, to working with fillers and fiberglass, to the tricks of flawless custom painting. It's all here in straightforward, easy-to-follow text and photographs by the one women who loves it and does it best, "Crazy Horse" JoAnn Bortles.

I hope this book inspires you as it has me.

—Hank Young, Young Choppers and Hot Rods Inc.
(www.youngchoppers.com)

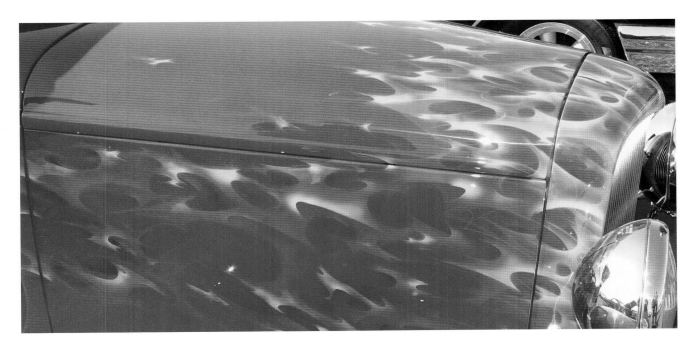

INTRODUCTION

To look down my driveway now, there is no clue to the fact that I once owned 20 Ford Mustangs, several classic Jaguars (including a 1966 XKE), and a 1968 Cougar GT E, all at the same time. I moved a lot, and my landlords did not like me. These days I own killer custom bikes. They take up much less space, but hot rod cars still are, and always have been, in my blood.

In 1976 I turned 16 years old. Two months before my 16th birthday, I bought a 1969 Mustang for $550. The afternoon after I got my driver's license, my dad picked up my best friend MaryAnn and me and dropped us off at the car. We drove it off the lot and into the first of what would be many adventures in that car. I did most of the mechanical work on that car but knew almost nothing about bodywork or paintwork.

I was always interested in cars. I was drawing cars long before I ever drove any. My contribution to my high school art calendar was a 1957 Chevy. In fact, the painting that got me accepted at Parson's School of Design was of a race car. Although I had only painted pictures of cars at this point, it only seemed natural that my art would find its way onto the surface of an automobile.

Then in 1981 I bought a rusted-out 1966 Mustang coupe. In fact, the car was so rusted out the owner did not even want to sell it to me. I learned fiberglass work, how to cut off and weld on body panels, and how to paint a car. I painted it white, the perfect color to hide bad—I mean, "less than perfect"—bodywork. But the end result was worth all the effort. It looked like a completely different car.

The white 1966 became my daily driver. It took me on long cross-country trips from Connecticut to Illinois, Georgia, and all over the East Coast for a number of years.

Then all the "trouble" started. Along with two friends, I rented a small shop in the rough end of town and proceeded to accumulate and paint Mustangs. A 1968 Cougar proved

An oil painting of a Formula 1 car.

An airbrush painting I did of my first car.

A pen and ink drawing of a 1957 Chevy I did for my high school art calendar.

My first Mustangs were painted in the backyard.

to be the biggest challenge, as it was the first car I would paint black. Black is a difficult color to paint, as it shows every flaw in the bodywork.

My Cougar GTE XR7 was a very rare car. It came with a 427 side-oiler motor and was one of only 256 ever made. So I wanted it to be as perfect as possible. It was the first time I had ever painted a car indoors with the overhead door closed. I didn't use a respirator (not smart), and I stumbled out of the shop completely groggy from paint fumes. When the fumes and my head cleared, I saw that every little imperfection in the bodywork showed. Even though I had a near flawless coat of clear over the black, it made no sense to have exquisite clear over less than perfect bodywork. I took out my flatboard and proceeded to work down the sides of the car.

The third car I would own. Wish I still had it.

My 1968 Cougar GTE Eliminator 427. I loved that car.

Another view of my beloved Cougar.

I reprimed and resanded until I was sure it was perfect. And the second time I applied the black, I watched as the paint laid out on an incredibly unflawed body.

There would be no custom paint on my first cars. Well, nothing that would be thought of as custom. I simply wanted those paint jobs to bring out the best features of these cars. Then I hit overload and suddenly had a yard full of rare and unreal cars, including a 1966 XKE Jaguar. Too

many cars, too many projects. My latest landlord was having heart failure, and I ended up selling nearly everything, including the Cougar. I kept only my first 1966 Mustang, the white car. (By the way, if anyone knows the whereabouts of that Cougar, let me know.)

My next car project was a 1966 Pontiac Bonneville in 1989. It would be my first time painting a custom color on a car. The body was not in bad shape, so I went with a dark color. I wanted a deep color that lit up and glowed when the sun hit it. I began with a black base coat, then mixed candy turquoise with blue pearl and applied a bunch of layers of that. The result was a rich, bottomless, dark turquoise that turned purple when viewed from different angles. And wherever the light hit it, it glowed brightly as if lit up. I had achieved what I wanted it to do. It showed the unreal killer results that can be obtained when a painter thinks outside the paint chip chart and gets creative.

The Bonneville would be my last personal car project (so far). The truly killer car paint projects wouldn't start up for another 10 years. By then my paint skills had considerably improved. And thanks to hooking up with a great shop like Little Rock Auto Body of Charlotte, North Carolina, my car painting has been winning awards at huge car shows, beating out hundreds of competitors.

The reason? It takes more than talent to successfully

My 1966 Pontiac Bonneville.

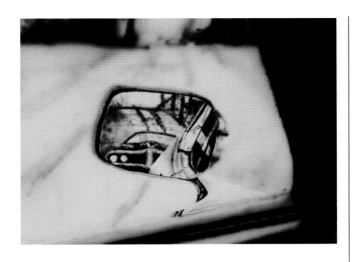

This early airbrush painting features two cars from my teen years: the 1968 Firebird of my high school friend Sherri as seen from the side view mirror of my 1970 Mustang.

paint cars. It helps to have a good crew for support. I don't have a downdraft paint booth, but Little Rock does. And whatever answers I don't possess, chances are their painters, Wayne and Jimmy Springs, can provide them. And whenever we don't know something between the three of us, we can figure it out or fake it. Painting cars is best approached as a team effort. You can do it all yourself, but it helps to have friends. Especially since painting cars involves quite a bit of disassembly and reassembly.

Every car is different and each one has its own set of problems. So it's best to do research on whatever car or truck you're working on. And try to find the local expert, as there will be questions that will come up. Of course, the easiest way is to hook up with a good body shop and only contract to do the actual custom paint work itself. Some custom painters hire people who specialize in car assembly and basic painting.

When first diving into a car painting project, it can seem overwhelming. There are always so many details that are overlooked until deep into the project. That's when it will feel like you'll be 90 years old and still working on that stupid car. Yes, there will be times when the painter will hate the vehicle being worked on. You'll feel that if you have to look at it one more day, you'll go completely insane. It's never as easy as it looks. And if it looks like an easy project, that's the one that will make you want to drive off a cliff.

Always give yourself extra time and money for a project. If you're new to painting cars, double the amount of time and money you've budgeted for the project. Hey, if you have money left over after the car is done, throw a party for all those who helped. You'll be ready for one, believe me.

Me with one of the greatest, yet most humble, talents in automotive art, Chuck Mack. Chuck has worked with companies like Hendrick Motorsports. Chuck's drawings and designs have always been an inspiration to me. He is actually responsible for teaching me how to draw out my artwork designs on vehicles and bring them to life. Thanks Chuck!

CHAPTER 1
THE BASICS AND OTHER "BORING" STUFF

Paradise for a custom painter is painting a body that's been removed from the frame. There are two reasons why this is so: First off, a car body mounted on a rolling jig is easy to move around. You can quickly roll it over to where the light is better or swing the body around to work on the other side. The second and main reason is that there is very little to tape off and no engine or chrome to worry about getting hit by overspray. There's no interior to deal with, no glass, no wires, no nothing! But this is not a perfect world and most cars you'll be working on will require hours of preparation for painting.

So here are what I call the rules for custom painting cars. It sounds serious when I say it that way, and I try to take a lighthearted approach to painting, but wasting time and money (and endangering your sanity) can be a serious business. Jimmy Springs, one of the best painters I know, jokes about his hatred of painting cars, motorcycles, and boats, especially boats. By following these rules, maybe I can save you from a real hatred of painting.

THE RULES

1. When in doubt, start over! Too many hours are wasted by trying to salvage a ruined paint job. If the paint wrinkles, lifts, bubbles, or does anything that has you ready for smelling salts or scratching your head wondering where you went wrong, head for the heavy grit sandpaper, or in some cases the sandblaster, and start over. I have made some great saves in this department (see Chapter 15), but I have squandered far too much time on questionable paint jobs. These hours would have been better spent on a paint job I didn't have to worry about down the road. I knew my mistake, knew how to avoid it again, and should have started over. If I had, I wouldn't have to worry about the phone ringing and hearing a customer say, "What is this little mark in my paint? It seems to be growing."

2. The best offense is a good defense. This holds true in painting, from making sure you have a solid foundation under all those beautiful top coats to little things like having plenty of clear coat over your base coats. The big advantage being that if the artwork is in some way less than desirable, you can simply remove the artwork by wet sanding it off with 600-grit and then start over, saving the base paint. Of course, if liquid stencil mask was used for the artwork, then there may be slight lines from cutting the stencil. But plenty of clear coat will allow you to sand most of those lines away and maybe cover the rest with retouching.

Don't let this happen to you! Don't become a car hater-painter!

This pristine 1955 Chevy is an example of what happens when a painter does not take shortcuts. Jimmy Springs, painter at Little Rock Auto Body of Charlotte, North Carolina, removed nearly every panel from this car. Then he stripped each one down to bare metal, then primed and filled any imperfections until the surfaces were flawless. The body of this car does not have the tiniest ripple. Of course, during the process, it did get frustrating. But when that black paint went on and Jimmy saw that all his careful work was justified, he got that buzz that comes from seeing the great result of those long hours before the top coats get sprayed.

3. Shortcuts suck, and they never work. A good foundation and proper paint processes will save your life. You'll worry less and have fewer problems to deal with because you did things the right way. Stress kills, or at least it seems like you're dying. Most custom painters are self-employed. They carry the whole load when something goes wrong. To shut down the shop and go home at a decent hour is one of the best experiences there is, especially after suffering through too many torturous long nights into the morning hours due to mistakes. Painting cars is a whole lot more than just walking up to a vehicle with airbrush in hand and starting to spray. Planning and research go into each paint job. And once that is finished, more research is done to test colors and artwork techniques. Many times drawings will be made up to see how the ideas work on a car or truck. Then the vehicle must be prepped, which can add hours to the job the painter might not have figured on.

This is not the time for shortcuts. Paint will not stick to an improperly sanded surface and will easily chip off during reassembly, buffing, or cleaning. Problem areas here tend to be around the edges of panels. No matter how sick you are of sanding on that car, do not paint over any areas that still have shine to them! You'll be a whole lot sicker when paint starts flaking from those areas. And it will! Believe me. Don't take shortcuts.

4. Clean your paint gun. No matter how beat you are, no matter how late it is, if it's 2 a.m. and you've been at it since 7 in the morning, give that gun a thorough cleaning before you shut down the shop.

5. Test your color and artwork techniques, and save your butt. This is one of the biggest mistakes even a good experienced painter can make. In most cases, I make sample pieces with color and artwork choices. I'll use junk panels or sign blanks which are available at sign supply stores online. Also, look for junk parts like hoods and trunk lids in the junk pile at any body shop. Chances are if you are painting cars you know someone who works at a body shop. Ask them if you can pick through their junk pile.

The House of Kolor Tangelo Pearl seen here is a perfect example of why it's a good idea to check colors and to paint them on sunny days. No way this color shows this much spark and glow on a cloudy day. Paint by Ryan Young, Indocil Art

For instance, say I need to spray a red flake. I'll do several test panels trying out base coat and candy coat combos, varying the kind of base flake I use and the amounts of candy toner I use in the top coat. I take notes on how much toner I add each time, the type of flake I'm using, and how many coats I go through. When I produce a sample that works, I can simply copy the formula on the real part. This way there are no surprises after you've sprayed 10 coats of material. Making it up as you go doesn't often have a happy ending. Fine-tune your paint to get the most effective result. Always know your choices and then let your customer choose the one they prefer. Make a recommendation but let them make the final choice. And always get proof, like an e-mail or signed note. That way, at payment time, if they decide it's not the color they want, you don't eat the cost of changing it. (Note: I broke this rule during one of the paint jobs in this book and was sick over it.)

6. Wash your hands. Many pesky paint surface problems are caused by the transfer of contaminants from hands. The natural oils produced by your skin can cause fingerprints that forever appear through layers and layers of paint and clear. Some painters wear gloves—latex, vinyl, or cotton. I cannot airbrush or wet sand in gloves. Try taping off parts while wearing gloves. Not me. I only wear gloves while spraying coats of paint in the booth or when I'm cleaning my equipment. All other times I am barehanded, but that can cause strange fingerprints that appear under the clear coat

months later. It is amazing the crap that gets caught between the ridges of fingerprints. I wash my hands as often as every 20 minutes when I'm laying out tape to cover chrome or other parts, or when I'm taping off flames or custom graphics. I also wash up each time before I wet sand. Using a mild liquid soap along with lots of rinsing gets the best results. I'm not as picky when I spend my time airbrushing, as I don't touch the surface that much with my fingers.

Any time your hands are touching a painted surface they must be totally free of any oils. Hands also pick up oils from touching skin, so I keep a long-handled artist's paintbrush near my workbench to use as an itch scratcher. I always keep cotton swabs around to clean my airbrushes and they work great for little ear itches. In the winter, all that washing can be a little hard on the hands, but it's harder on my nerves when tape pulls loose because it was laid over an oily spot or when I discover the whitish glow of a nice neat fingerprint against what I thought was a flawless black surface.

Keep a pump container of liquid soap right there at the sink. Also, use a clean washcloth to hold onto parts while you're wet sanding them. When handling dry parts, use paper towels between your hands and the painted surface. My skin very seldom touches a wet or ready-to-spray painted surface. Too many hard lessons in this area.

7. Try not to paint custom colors on cloudy days. Yet, in many cases, nighttime painting is the only option. If you have a lot of evenly distributed light in your painting

area, you can paint anytime. I only mention this as it's an easy way to reduce painting errors. I try not to spray any color on anything but a sunny day. Reason? After the paint is dry to the touch, if possible, I like to check the color in the sun. I've even rolled cars out of the spray booth to check the color. If I'm painting black, I'll be able to tell if any little bits of pearl or metallic from a previous job have landed in the paint. With custom colors, I check the part against the color sample I made, seeing if the color is correct or if I need another coat of paint. I've tried electric natural lights, portable halogens, and all kinds of artificial light, only to find later on that I needed to do things differently after I saw the parts in direct sunlight. So now I don't take chances. I wait for a sunny day no matter how much the customer is yowling. They howl louder once their buddies start pointing out inconsistencies in their paint.

Any flaw or defect that doesn't show up in the direct sunlight will show up on cloudy days, especially color banding from improperly applied pearl paint. Too few coats of pearl can also cause this. So before doing artwork over your base coat, know for certain that it is correct; check it in sunlight, indirect light, and artificial light, as most indoor auto shows will have that kind of light. Beware, because when the color looks great in the booth light, chances are when you look at it in the direct sunlight you'll find you need to apply one more coat. My painting buddies tease me about it, but it's worth the effort.

8. Read through each chapter before you try using the process it details. This is not a painting rule, just good common sense when using this book. Underline

HANDY HINT

Before you mix any paint, check your materials. Make sure you're pouring primer catalyst into that primer, not clear coat catalyst. On the same hand, make sure it is precleaner you're about to wipe those parts down with, not base coat clear or reducer. Containers often look alike. Double-check everything, especially when working late at night or when under pressure from deadlines. Keep a clean, uncluttered paint bench and set out all the stuff you'll be using so you're not blindly reaching into a cabinet as you mix. If you're mixing up something and it doesn't look "right" or you open a container and it looks odd (this especially pertains to catalyst), stop. Don't use it. Check your materials, and if they look right, mix up a smaller batch. If it does the same thing, test it on a sample part and/or call your paint dealer and ask questions.

or mark parts that you want to really remember when you are using the process. And if boo-boos crop up, don't panic or freak out. Just calmly research the problem by reading the tech sheet on the product you are using, and by checking the chapter in this book that deals with that process (and the Troubleshooting chapter). And don't be afraid to ask the opinions of other painters. Chances are they have been there and know a little trick that will save you.

EQUIPMENT

If you start with substandard equipment, chances are good you'll get a substandard paint job. Those paint guns I threw against the wall 25 years ago? They were all cheapo guns or used-to-death stuff that should have hit the trash heap long before I got to them. A good quality paint gun and filtering equipment is money well spent. With proper care, quality equipment will last many years. Although my absolute preference is the SATA line of equipment, most top-of-the-line spray gun manufacturers make guns and equipment that will do the work for you as well and may be your preference.

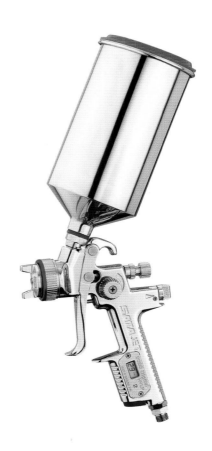

The SATAjet 2000 Digital HVLP. My favorite all purpose spray gun.

Spray Guns

Quality equipment is not inexpensive. But you have to ask yourself: Is it worth it? As you're standing there, cheapo gun in hand, looking at that blob of old paint that just came out of the nozzle and ruined the perfect coat of candy apple paint you were admiring just a moment ago, was saving a few bucks worth it? Now you've set yourself back by a day or more, not counting the wasted material.

Or suddenly the airflow or the paint flow ain't flowing like it was yesterday or a moment ago. Now you've got to stop, pour out the paint, pull the gun apart, and look for the cause of the problem. You could have been done, cleaned up, and on your way out the door.

Can't afford that gun? How much is your time worth? But don't listen to me; use crap guns like I did and suffer. When a paint job is ruined by a bad gun, you'll give anything to turn back the clock and use a quality spray gun. With the obscenely high cost of paint and painting materials, can you afford not to use a good spray gun?

SATA makes the perfect guns for any kind of painting, especially motorcycle and auto painting, from the top-of-the-line SATAjet 2000 HVLP DIGITAL 2 to the RP DIGITAL 2. The RP's heavy spray is perfect for clear coating. With their digital readout right there on the handle, the painter can perfectly dial in the optimum air pressure.

I used to use old junk guns for priming, and I paid the price in extra time sanding. A smooth and evenly applied coat of primer is very essential for saving time. A uniformly applied round of primer will save time in the sanding phase and provide a smoother surface for color coating.

Filtering Equipment

It's no use having premium guns and using high-dollar paint if the air going through the gun and carrying the paint onto the surface is dirty. I've seen crap blow out of guns with all kinds of air dryers and such in the system.

You need a quality filtering system right in your booth or no more than 50 feet away from the gun. SATA's 0/444 modular system of lined-up filters makes it easy. The first filter precleans down to 5 microns. The second stage filter goes down to 0.01 micron. The setup even includes two outlets, one for your gun hose and one for an air-supplied respirator. More about that in the safety section.

Why spend money to take so many precautions? Like I said, time is money. The horrible thing is, chances are you won't know something has gone wrong until the last coat has been sprayed. You take a look the next morning and see problems, and after wasting a morning or a day chasing down the cause, you find it could have been

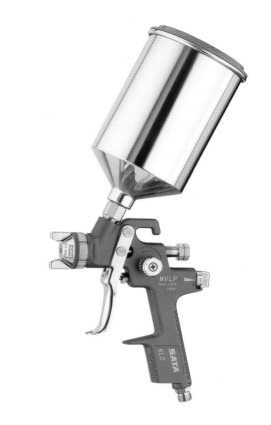

SATA's KLC, HVLP, and KLC RP primer guns.

SATA's 0/444 modular filter system.

Three Very, Very Handy Tools

Above left: *This little goodie is a dual-action random orbital sander. It has a palm grip and is very lightweight. These are not cheap and good ones retail for about $150. You want to get one that is light. You can comfortably use one of these all day. The 3M Hook-It system is a line of easy-to-use sandpaper discs and backing pads. The pad has a Velcro-like pad and the sanding discs "hook" right on. Use the 180-grit to take down old paint and bodywork. The 320 works great for prepping painted surfaces for priming or sealing. Use 800 for intercoat work and 1500 for post painting and rubbing out dust prior to buffing. This will make a several hour task take less than one hour.* **Above right:** *This eraser pad will remove all vinyl pinstriping, graphics, and adhesive residue without damaging the paint. Just mount the eraser in an air drill and go easy on the speed. Keep it low and easy. If used properly, it will safely remove all the old body striping in minutes. Unlike chemicals and solvents commonly used for this job, the soft wheel is gentle to most finishes. Take extreme care if using on any non-metal surface, like plastic. It will heat up the surface and can damage the plastic. Eastwood Tools sells these for less than $15.00.*

Masking machines and tree-style masking stations are extremely handy to have around. Mount a roll of narrow, medium, and long masking paper and attach the end of a roll of tape to each one. This will make short work of masking a vehicle for painting, for artwork, for anything. Prices vary depending on manufacturer, from $60 to $200.

avoided if only the proper equipment had been used. I have been there.

At the very least, get a good quality water separator. A water separator does just what its name says. It removes water from the air system. It should be mounted right in your booth or no more than 50 feet away from the gun.

Air Compressors

Over the years I have found that if you're doing anything other than light airbrushing (that is, using spray guns) it is best to have a compressor with a storage tank. For many years, I used a 5-horsepower, single-cylinder compressor with a 25-gallon tank. It provided plenty of air pressure for painting small parts, and it plugged into a standard 110 outlet.

But painting cars and using air tools like grinders and sanders can drain down the tank quickly. An even better choice is a 7.5–10-horsepower two-stage air compressor.

SAFETY

Do not store paint in the basement or in an attached garage. It is a horrible fire and health hazard, all those fumes. It just takes one spark. I store my paint in a detached shed. Over-

SATA's fresh air system.

all, never do spray work in the basement or closed garage. Very bad idea.

I painted for several years before using a fresh-air-supplied respirator and slowly poisoned myself. Painters don't die of old age, and I want as many years as I can get. I had been thinking about getting a fresh air system for years. But I always had an excuse: too bulky, too expensive, dragging around all those hoses, etc. Then after spending an entire day in the booth I woke up feeling like crap. I felt like I had food poisoning and I knew why. What bothered me even more was that this had happened many times before, but I always shrugged it off and toughed it out. Being tough is being there to provide for your family. Coughing and dying young because you were stubborn is not tough.

When SATA came out with their new fresh air system, I had no more excuses. One hose supplies air and quickly and easily disconnects from the small carbon filter belt unit. The helmet is very lightweight and comes with replaceable tear-off sheets for the visor. There's no separate compressor, and no heavy hoses dragging around. No more waking up sick.

I'll be nervous the rest of my life about all those isocyanates I've inhaled through my traditional respirator. If I could go back in time and use a fresh air system, I would. I'd pay whatever the price, but I would never risk shortening

my life again. And yes, it is more fun to spend money on new wheels but it's also good to stick around for a good long time to enjoy those wheels. It's well worth it. Don't take chances. Life is way too short as it is. Go get that respirator.

I also wear a paint suit and gloves in the booth. I never let any solvents get on my skin. If they do, I wash and dry them off immediately. If I get paint on my skin I use a product like 3M's Paintbuster to wash it off. I never use thinner or reducer to wash my hands. When cleaning anything with solvents, I use SAS Vinyl Guard Gloves. I hate latex. Derma-Lite Nitrile gloves are also very solvent resistant.

Never breathe the chemicals used for cleaning a spray gun. They will kill you. If I am doing any painting other than light airbrushing I wear an air-supplied respirator. For airbrushing, I wear a small cartridge style respirator. One trick, when not in use, is to remove the cartridges and put each one in a small Ziploc bag. The bigger the storage bag, the more air is trapped inside the bag. Oxygen is what depletes the chemical filtration materials.

OK, I'll stop preaching and get to the fun parts.

BEWARE OF TOO THICK PAINT

The insane irony of custom paint on cars is that, in numerous cases, many layers of paint will be applied. The problem comes when parts such as trim, door handles, and other hardware will bolt against those heavily layered surfaces, squashing down the paint and causing it to lift and bubble.

The remedy? Know where parts will bolt against the surface. Try to keep the paint in those areas as thin as possible, including primer. And always make sure those areas get sanded thoroughly so the paint will stick well. Some colors, like candy, are impossible to spray lightly in certain areas, since the color needs to be evenly distributed. But primer and clear coats can be manipulated to accommodate problem areas.

Also, check the clearances between panels, such as the space between the fenders and doors. How much room is there for a zillion candy coats? You want those spaces to be nice and even.

SURFACE PREPARATION

Before starting any paint job, if parts are being replaced, check over the new parts when picking them up: First to make sure they are the correct parts, and second to make sure the parts are in good shape. When I restored my 1966 Mustang in 1981, I rejected two sets of new fenders before taking the third set. The reason? The fenders came in black primer and it was easy to sight down the length of the fenders and see they were not very straight. I found a few small dings and other imperfections. Why create more work for yourself?

I painted this 1970 Mustang back in the early 1980s. It needed quite a bit of surface prep.

HANDY HINT

Time spent in the spray booth can make things murky without you realizing it. You can be staring straight at a problem and not see it. Taking time away from the booth and literally "airing" out your system will help your senses. After time away from the booth, step back in it to check out your work. Half the time you'll see something that you missed or something you need to fix before you can proceed. I use a SATA air-supplied system, but I still take a little break in between coats of paint.

Check the paint manufacturer's recommendations for the window of time each coat needs to dry and the amount of time the surface can sit before recoating. Use that time to get some fresh air and to carefully inspect your work.

Flames will be painted on the firewall of this 1939 Ford. The rest of the car is masked off with tape and plastic.

Before the parts are permanently installed, this is the time to fill any trim holes or do any kind of work to the car. Make sure the gaps between panels are even, adjust hoods and trunk lids to make sure they open and close properly. When there are 19 coats of flawless paint, that's not the time to try and find out why the hood doesn't latch completely.

This book deals with acrylic urethane base coats and urethane clear enamels, not lacquer. Although there are painters who still work exclusively with lacquer, I no longer use it. I used to swear by it and couldn't imagine using anything else. But it started getting hard to find, so

I switched to the urethane enamels. I airbrush with base coat enamel, but all my primers, candy, and clear coats are done in two-part mixes.

Some painters use an etching primer before they apply the filler primer. I like for paint to have a good "tooth" to bite to. Many times, parts that come in bare metal have an oily coating. I wash the metal down with lacquer thinner, in some cases you would then sandblast the parts. I use an etching primer when sandblasting is not an option.

For overall refinish spraying over existing paint, wash down the surface with a strong precleaner until it squeaks. Then, if using a palm or random (no handle) dual-action sander, go over the surface with 320. Do not use a regular (with handle) DA sander to take down a surface, as it may leave swirl marks. Or wet sand with 220-grit wrapped around a block by hand. Next, apply two-part epoxy primer and then two-part primer over the paint surface.

PREPPING FIBERGLASS AND PLASTIC PARTS

Never sandblast plastic or fiberglass parts! Wet sand them down with 320-grit or Media Blast which will not leave the plastic fuzz that sanding does. You don't want the scratches to be too deep. I like to wet sand whenever possible. I like the smooth surface that it leaves. Sand scratches can be a real problem with fiberglass or hard plastic parts so I try to get a good tooth on the surface without creating deep scratches that will come back to haunt me through five coats of previously flawless candy paint.

After sanding, they are ready for epoxy primer and base coat color. For certain parts like bumpers that have a slight flex to them, like polypropylene, you'll need to use a special clear primer made specifically for those parts. Whatever brand of paint system you are using will have a product that is made for painting on flexible or black plastic parts. Dust two coats of that on, and then apply your two-part primers.

After applying and sanding primer coats, and right before spraying color coats, I spray on a quick-drying sealer. House of Kolor's Ko-Seal II Primer Sealer is perfect for this. Ko-Seal comes in three colors: white, black, and metallic. If the basecoat color will be black, a black sealer coat means less coats of base black will need to be sprayed to cover. The metallic sealer will require less metallic color basecoats. Some painters even use the metallic sealer as a basecoat for their candy or custom color coats.

PPG's DP50LF epoxy sealer consists of two parts epoxy primer, one part catalyst (DP402LF), and 1/2 part reducer (DT reducer). PPG's epoxy primer comes in five colors, designated by a two-digit number. This seals the surface in case there are sand-throughs down to the metal and/or through the various layers of primer. It also helps to smooth over any deep sand scratches. Watch out for paint piling up on the edges of panels, and sand off any excess material.

Now you're ready for color coats.

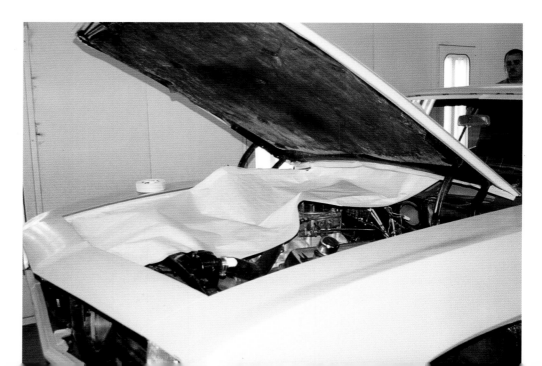

Don't take shortcuts when it come to taping off areas like the engine, trunk, door jams, etc. It can actually take longer to prep these areas than to spray the paint. But proper prep is one of the things that will set one painter apart from the rest. Thoroughly wipe out the channels around the trunk and engine compartment and tape those off.

ONE LAST THING ABOUT BODY PREP

Here is a 1968 Camaro properly prepared for paint. The wheels have been removed and the car is up on jacks, to allow for access. The wheel wells have been completely taped off. No overspray will be on the black undercoat they received. The bumpers have been removed. The door handles and door locks are removed and their mounting holes taped from the inside of the door. The grill, windshield, rally lights, and turn signal mounting holes have been taped off.

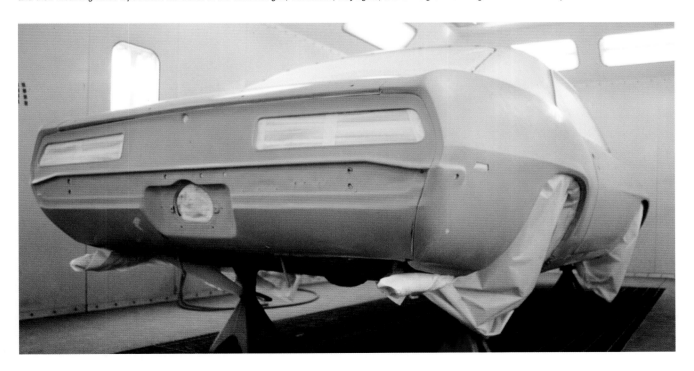

A view of the Camaro from the rear. The taillights, gas cap access hole, running light mounting holes, windows, and even the tail pipes have been taped off. This is hours of prep here. It is so tempting to take shortcuts during prep. Don't. Your work will reflect it.

CHAPTER 2
THE HARSH REALITIES OF PAINTING CUSTOM BASE COATS

Here's the biggest truth about custom painting cars and trucks: They are big and will use up a great deal of paint.

Paint these days is unbelievably costly. Bad planning and bad painting will result in unimaginable nightmares. Take the time to plot out your painting strategy. Unfamiliar with a product or the equipment being used? Test your colors on a small piece of metal first. Know as much as you can about what you are about to do. Knowledge is power and will save you from sitting there feeling sick from looking at the results of $500 worth of painting materials and countless hours down the drain.

I've already gone over the rules in the previous chapter. And once you apply common sense to your painting methods, you take most of the guesswork out of it. Always read the tech sheets on the paint product you are using. They'll

HANDY HINT

Always make sure there is plenty of light in the paint booth. In order to get even coverage when painting, look for a reflection of light on the surface being painted. Watch the flow as the paint hits the surface and move the gun accordingly. I never make a final decision on the number of coats on the surface or on my final color without taking a break away from the booth. Once you're done, go have lunch, clear your head, then go back and check your color.

Paint often changes color slightly as it dries. This is why you need to know your material. The product sheet will tell you what kind of window (time between coats or time to recoat without resanding) you have.

This pickup is a great example of how the right color can bring a vehicle to life. Truck painted and owned by Jimmy Springs.

Basic black sure looks great on this 1955 Chevy. Paint by Jimmy Springs

recommend things like how many coats should be applied, the overlap of coats you'll need, air pressures, how long to wait between coats, and much more. If you didn't get a product sheet when you bought your paint, go online and see if you can download one from the company's website. And try to read the Material Safety Data Sheets (MSDS) sheets as well. They tell you about the product you are using, its compound contents, and using it safely. They also tell you (sometimes) what they work well with and what they don't. And ask your paint dealer regularly if there are updates.

House of Kolor (HOK) even has a tech manual that extensively details how to use all their products. I still find myself hauling out that manual, even though I've been using their products for over 20 years. I have "painter's memory," and I do not always remember how a product behaves. Even if you've been painting for years, when you run into a problem and need a quick answer, that tech info can come in very, very handy.

My method of laying down coats of paint is simple. I spray one coat in one direction, say horizontally. Then I run the next coat up and down vertically. I'll run the following coat diagonally. This way I get total coverage with no color bands, or lines of darker color, running through the job. It tends not to be a big problem with solid nonmetallic colors, but with pearl or candy colors it can be a pesky problem, especially if you don't apply enough coats.

THE TWO-GUN SOLUTION

Try to have two spray guns to use for top coats, one for pearls, most solid colors, and metallics, and one for black, white, candy, and clear. It's better to have three guns, one for primer only. But if all you can afford is one gun you'll have to keep it super clean because bits of pearl and primer get stuck in the gun and make an appearance the next time black is sprayed through it. I use cotton swabs to wipe out the interior of the gun after the nozzle and needle are removed and also wiped clean.

I have a primer gun, one for pearls/metallics, one for solid colors, a candy/black gun, and a clear coat gun.

I carefully choose base coat colors that will complement the artwork that will be done. Give yourself some time to think about it. What color will bring out the best features of the car? The 1939 Ford on the cover of this book was the subject of much long torment and speculation about what color to use. The customer wanted the car to have impact. We looked at golds, pearl tangerines, all kinds of red pearls, and then I talked him into painting the car black. The main reason was the car had what could be an awkward shape if painted the wrong color. By painting the car black and airbrushing bright yellow and orange flames on the front end, the large rear section of the car became more balanced with the front of the car. This combination of colors brought out the best features and made the lines of the car flow better.

I like to look through paint books and other resources to find interesting colors. Then I have to talk a customer into using it. I've gotten some strange looks over the colors I choose, but every time I've been able to use some funky color the result is perfect. Whatever color you choose, it is a good idea to keep track of what you use and the number of coats applied. I have a file for every paint job and try to put as much info on that paint job as possible in the folder. Maybe I'll just scrawl on the outside of a folder, "3 coats silver base, 5 coats blue candy: clear mixed with concentrate med dark." I usually do this when I'm making my sample piece.

And keep track of the temperature in and around your work area. If the car or part you're painting was just moved from a colder section of the shop or from outside, and your booth or spray area is warmer, give the parts some time to heat up. Painting cold parts in a warm area with warm paint can result in crazing or cracking.

Look through paint charts but don't allow yourself to be limited to colors straight out of the "can." There are many different ways to play around with creating custom colors. You can lay down a few coats of pearl, and then layer some candy over it. Maybe mix some pearl into the candy. Do a few layers of candy paint with pearl, then a few layers of straight candy. Maybe spray on a coat of HOK Wild Cherry Kandy, then a coat of HOK Kandy Brandywine.

As for the best spray gun to use, some painters prefer a regular pressure gun like SATA's RP. I like using HVLP guns like SATA's 2000. It lays down an even application of paint and I'm used to the way it sprays. If you're using multiple spray guns, that's another statistic to keep track of so you can repeat a successful procedure on multiple parts.

The best advice I can give on painting custom colors? Practice. Before painting any custom color, if you're not used to doing it, test the color on a spare or junk piece of metal. You won't just be testing the color. You'll be testing how your gun sprays that color. How fast you need to move the gun. The optimum air pressure for that kind of paint. How the color appears as it's being painted in the light of your spray area. Lighting is very important. Knowing how

your spray gun sprays the color is critical. Don't wait until after the first coat is sprayed to find that you have questions.

Testing custom colors prior to spraying the car will bring up questions. And more testing will answer those questions. You'll be a better painter for it.

PEARL COLORS

This step-by-step follows a pearl paint application. When it comes to pearl colors, undercoat painting can determine the intensity of the finished product. Pearl color comes either premixed, such as House of Kolor's PBC Shimrin line of pearls, or in a powder or paste form that can be mixed with clear base coat or clear urethane. You can also mix powder or paste pearl in with nearly any color. Looking for a dark base coat, almost black, but want the color to light up where the sunlight hits it? Go with a black undercoat, then dust a bit of pearl on the car. Try and use the same color pearl as the end result color, like purple pearl for a purple-tinted color. Then follow that with a few coats of candy in the end result color. Keep in mind the more pearl that is used, the brighter the color will be. Don't use too much candy, as the more pearl and candy you use, the less black it will be.

Looking for a pearl so bright it hurts your eyes? Lay down a bright white base coat and apply the pearl coats over that. The car will have a glow to it. Another trick is to mix pearl into solid colors such as red, use that as a base and layer a few coats of candy over it. Always use a wide gun pattern to spray pearls or metallics. Don't go too dry with your coats. Lay them on smooth and flat. Try to keep a gun distance of 8 inches from the surface and use a 75 percent pattern overlap.

Pearl color comes either premixed, such as House of Kolor's PBC Shimron line of pearls, or in a powder or paste form that can be mixed with clear basecoat or clear urethane. You can also mix powder or paste pearl with nearly any color.

HANDY HINT

One thing to watch out for when spraying pearl paint is color banding. It appears as bands of darker color across the painted surface and can be hard to see in direct sun but shows up very well in the shade or indoors. This can be caused by an uneven pattern on the spray gun, not using enough coats, improper overlap, spraying too close to the surface, or not changing spray gun direction with each coat. Improper air pressure can also cause this.

Splotching uneven areas of color can also occur. This is usually caused by not spraying enough coats.

Pearl should be applied in medium coats. Not too light as it will tend to get a grainy, hairy, bumpy, or orange peely texture. If your gun is spraying too dry or you're holding the gun too far away; you'll also get a bumpy surface to the pearl. You'll lose that endless depth effect that is desired.

If you do see a bumpy surface building up, stop painting. Let it dry overnight and wet sand with 600. Start over by repainting the black or white undercoat. If the pearl is applied too heavy, the pearl will mottle and run together.

Some areas receive more paint than other areas and "dark" streaks appear throughout the panel. Hoods and roofs are especially prone to this since they're hard to view from the right angle. This problem may not been easily seen in booth light or sunlight. But it will show up in the shade, under indirect light, or on a cloudy day. Test the gun's pattern on a piece of paper taped to the booth wall prior to painting. Make sure it is even throughout the pattern. If not, remove the aircap, needle and nozzle. Clean the paint and air passages and make sure there is no old paint obstructing the paint flow.

This dark pink pearl was a strange choice for this street rod but with the yellow flames, it makes perfect sense.

One of the wildest colors I'd seen in a while was an intense gold pearl I saw on a hot rod in Vegas. It was achieved by mixing HOK PBC47 Goldmine Pearl with HOK Kandy Basecoat KBC12 Pagan Gold.

Play around, experiment. That's what those spare parts are for. In addition to using them to gain experience with the equipment and material you are using, they can be a place to develop new ideas with color.

Color-changing pearl paint is applied over a black base coat for its most dramatic effect. House of Kolor's brand is called Kameleon. I find that three or four medium coats are all I need.

If this is your first time spraying pearls, experiment on a test panel first. Get used to the material. Paint is horribly expensive these days, and color-changing paints tend to run around $250 per eight ounces. So play it safe. Waste a little on a test panel instead of a lot on a whole set of sheetmetal.

Using the best gun for pearl application can also make a difference. An HVLP spray gun will break up the paint

3M Soft Edge Foam Masking Tape. This is a foam that has adhesive along one side. It sticks to and fills narrow areas like door jams, and trunk and hood edges. This is a real time saver. It will keep artwork overspray from getting into the door jams. I simply stick it along the edge and shut the door.

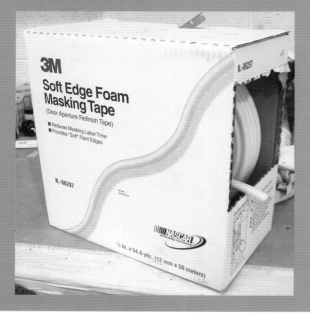

Don't forget to tack. The proper way to tack rag is to unfold the cloth and bunch it up. Then run it across the surface, scooping up any dust or debris. Don't press the cloth against the surface too hard. My favorite tack rag is Gerson Co. Blend Prep Tack Cloths. They are sticky without being too sticky. They work great for everything, but they are especially handy for tacking before painting urethanes. They aren't overly sticky, so there's no chance of leaving any residue behind. Their blue color makes them easy to tell apart from other tack rags.

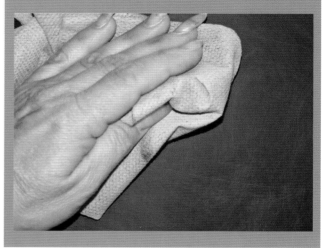

better than a regular pressure gun. The result is a more evenly dispersed spray of paint. The SATA 2000 HVLP is a very effective tool for stress-free pearl painting.

But there are some areas that will require a little more work than just sanding. Any damaged areas of the surface will be taken down with 320 on the DA or wet sanded with 400-grit, and the edges of the damaged areas feathered smooth.

Next, primer surfacer is applied to those areas and wet sanded with 600. Primer is softer than base coat, so 600-grit was used. The surface is now ready for a few coats of sealer. Never skip the sealer step. Sealer grabs down into the base, smooths over minor imperfections, provides a consistant color base and just plain gives the painter an easy to work on surface.

I'm going to take a Mazda Miata and wake it up a little. It actually has a good base of white to work from. There are several ways the first step can be done. I'll use a palm or random (no handle) dual action sander, go over the flat surface with 320 and use a red Scotch-Brite pad on the rest. Or the car can be wet sanded (wrap 800 grit paper around a soft block like Mequier's Hi-Tech Sanding Backing Pad). You don't want preparation scratches showing through the pearl. The pearl will lie down in the lines of the scratches.

Two coats of House of Kolor Ko-Seal II KS 10 white sealer have been sprayed on the car and now it's ready for the pearl. Use care when picking a white pearl basecoat. In certain kinds of light, pearl can have a tan or dark undertone that may not be desired. Note how the spoiler is mounted on two paint stands at the rear of the booth. Try to spray any small parts removed from the vehicle at the same time as the car. This especially pertains to painting candy paint.

Four coats of Snowwhite Pearl are applied. The first coat is sprayed up and down, the next one side to side, the next one diagonally, then the series is repeated if more coats are needed. I hold the gun about eight inches from the surface. I'm using a SATA 2000 digital HVLP spray gun. This little car will have the glow that the owner, Aaron Stevenson, wanted. Aaron took all the studio photographs seen in my books.

Laying down a white undercoat can make pearl colors truly glow. White undercoats can also make regular solid colors glow, like reds or blues. Whenever I spray yellow I always use a white undercoat. The reason for this is that yellow does not tend to cover well. There always seems to be a transparent effect with yellow. I'll spray a few coats of white, then a few coats of yellow.

HANDY HINT

When painting parts of the car, especially hoods, trunks, and doors, make sure to apply the paint to the edges. Make sure those edges look sharp before the customer sees they are not. Use care if spraying candy. You don't want dark borders around the edges of the doors, but the color needs to go around the sharp edge of the panels, not stop at the end of a flat surface. So check over those areas after the color coats are finished, turn down the gun pattern and pressure, maybe open up the door or trunk lid slightly and very carefully mist color if the edges are light.

We looked over white pearl color chips on a sunny day to find the best one. Then we looked at it in the shade. It stayed bright in the shade. Pearl whites with undertones looked darker in the shade but not in the sun. We decided on House of Kolor PBC-44 Snowhite Pearl.

The main thing to remember when spraying white is to make sure your spray gun is clean. What tends to happen is some nasty little bit of old paint will come out of the gun and land in the most visible part of the car. This always happens during the last coat. So take the gun apart and clean it thoroughly before spraying any very light color. Color banding (areas of poorly applied color) can happen easily with light pearls. But they are very hard to see in the paint booth. Make sure the coats are applied evenly and uniformly.

Clear coat will be applied next. I look pretty sexy in my SATA spray suit huh? After spraying any color, always apply a few coats of clear whether it is intercoat/base coat or urethane. This protects your base and gives you the surface you'll need to sand once you're ready for more coats or artwork. At this point, if artwork is not going over the basepaint, you may be able to get away with doing your finish clear coats. But I recommend wet sanding (with 600- or 800-grit sandpaper) the clear coats that were applied right after the basecoat color was painted. Don't overdo the sanding and go through the clear to the color coats. Just give the surface a smooth scuff down and knock down most of the orange peel areas. Now do your finish clear. Refer to Chapter 14 for further instructions.

Here is the new and improved Miata. But there's still work to be done. Ghost graphics will go on the lower portion of the sides. Refer to Chapter 9.

CANDY COLORS

Some painters insist the only way to spray candy is with pre-mixed candy urethane. Others prefer to mix candy concentrate or toner in base coat or urethane clear. Find what method and material works best for you. I like to use my favorite urethane clear and mix candy concentrate into that. This way I can play with the intensity of the candy tones.

Candy color application is basically like the pearl application, in that a metallic or pearl base coat is first applied, then candy color is layered over that. Metallic undercoats for candy are usually brighter than regular pearl bases, so they can reflect through the candy.

Many paint companies are getting into the custom color game. There are many choices of different colored undercoats for candy paint, the usual silver and gold but also tones of blue, green, purple, and many others. There are also many different metallics, some very fine, some big and bold, some in between. So take the time to do your research thoroughly and know your choices. With so many bases and the endless candy choices, you can get really wild.

But there are as many debates on the best way to apply candy as there are choices of color combos. I usually start out with lighter coats of candy, getting a nice even application of color using a 75 percent overlap. You want the candy to hit the surface in smooth, even coats but with none heavy enough to run or form sags. Once I have two medium coats applied, I add a bit more candy concentrate to my clear mix. As for how much concentrate to mix in the clear, I just do it by eye. I always mix my paint in plastic cups with measurements on them, like E-Z Mix plastic cups. After I mix up the candy, I stir it with an aluminum paint stick and check the intensity of the color by looking at the stick. It's better to go too light than too dark.

HANDY HINT

Watch out as you are spraying and take care not to lean into the side of the car as you are spraying the hood or the roof. Always watch where you are stepping as you make your way around the booth, especially when there are parts on stands in the booth with the car. You may brush against parts or the car without even realizing it.

Candy Red really brings out the angles on this car.

When mixing candies for strength or certain effects, use either a stainless steel or aluminum paddle. This gives you a constant color base to look at through the paint. It's best to be too light and add more concentrate. Too dark, and you'll end up with a stripe effect.

Like pearl paint application, I spray one coat up and down the length of the car or part, the next coat side to side, then diagonally, and so on. Always "walk" the car. Start your pass at one end and walk to the other, then move the gun down a little, and go back down the vehicle, concentrating on keeping the gun steady. Do not start and stop your pass at the end of each panel. Back and forth. Up and down. After applying a few coats this way, step back and judge whether or not it needs another pass or two. And try not to paint candy on a cloudy day, especially if you are a new painter. Judging the paint in the sunlight is essential, at least

One thing that can help keep the dust down especially in non downdraft paint booths, is to wet down the floor. I water it down after the car is in palce as it takes time to finish the taping and the water can begin to dry by that point. I don't use a hose as it can splash water onto the car. I carefully pour water onto the floor using a bucket, then with a floor squeegee or a broom, I push the water to cover the entire floor surface.

Great example of subtle, simple colors working together. The gold pearl paired with black is very, very effective. The orange graphic is minimal, but its impact is powerful. See how the pearl catches the light? The car just glows. This is Ryan Young's daily driver.

for me. Do not paint candy for the first time on a whole car! Paint a spare part first! It takes practice to spray candy without getting dark streaks on large surfaces.

Also take care not to run the paint around the bottom edges of the parts, especially the hood and trunk lid, as this causes a ridge on the edge. This can tend to be a real problem when applying candy paint, since trying to get the color smooth and even can often result in the coats going on too heavy. Urethane is used and it tends to flow out after the coat is applied. Gravity takes over and the urethane sags downward, building up on the fender edges.

As for the best spray gun to use for applying candy paint, some painters prefer a regular pressure gun like SATA's RP. It lays down an even thick surface. Myself and others like using HVLP guns like SATA's 2000. It thoroughly busts up the paint, lays a down an even application of paint and I'm used to the way it sprays. It all depends on what gun works most effectively for each painter.

I have very few photos of the 1966 Bonneville I owned in the mid 1980s and none truly show the the best feature of the paint. The color on this car was incredible. Yet, it was the result of a mistake. First I sprayed the car black. Then I had bought a bunch of turquoise candy color. But once I was ready to spray I realized there was no way I had enough paint. So I grabbed the most of whatever paint I had that was similar to mix in with the candy. This was in the lacquer days, so a painter could mix anything with anything. I had some blue murano star pearl, very rare stuff even then. I'd been saving it for a special paint job. I mixed it right into the candy, creating my own candy base coat in the process. Once I got the car in the sun, the color was wild. In the shade it looked dark purple/blue. But in the sun, the car lit up electric blue! Goes to show that you never know. You can go into the booth with one plan, disaster seems to happen, and you can end up with something unique and extreme.

CHAPTER 3
GETTING FLAKY WITH FLAKE PAINT

Back in the 1960s and 1970s flake paint was everywhere—on vans, cars, speedboats, and motorcycles. It was bold and brassy, the perfect base paint for the wild, experimental artwork that was being done at the time. Then it faded away. But over the past few years, custom painters are rediscovering flake paint and its endless possibilities.

Most paint companies have their own line of flake paint. Most of the time it comes dry in a jar and needs to be mixed with paint, usually clear paint. The flakes are made from very thin polyester and offered in different sizes from super brilliant and big to fine, a little bigger than pearl particles.

I like House of Kolor's line of flake. The colors are vibrant, and while the flake is brilliant, it's thin and lays down flat, requiring less clear to level out the surface. Their flakes range in size from 1/64-inch big flakes to 1/128-inch, the most popular size flake, and all the way down to 1/250- and 1/500-inch mini- and ultramini sizes.

MATERIAL AND EQUIPMENT
House of Kolor F-20 red flake
Course metallic basecoat color which is same tone as flake
House of Kolor KK-03 Wild Cherry Kandy Koncentrate
House of Kolor SG 100 Intercoat Clear
Urethane Clear
Reducer
Gerson Blend Prep Tack Cloths
EZ-Mix Cups
SATA 2000 Digital spray gun
SATA Agitator cup
SATA MiniJet 4
HOK Flake spoon

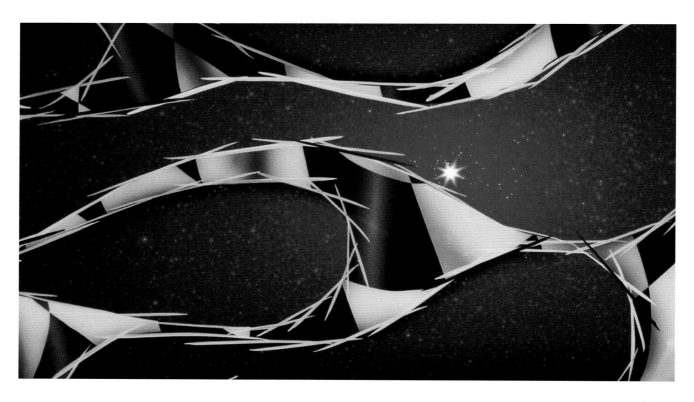

Red flake with candy apple red layered over it provides the perfect base for these flames.

I spray a black base coat on this hood.

Here's the main trick: Get out the coarsest base coat silver you have. If you are applying a gold flake, use the coarsest gold metallic available. If using a silver or colored flake, try HOK Orion Silver Shimrin BC02. If you're going with a colored flake, find the toner or dye that goes best with the colored flake. In this example, I'm using HOK F20 Red flake. KK01 Kandy Brandywine Koncentrate is very close in tone to the F20. Here I match the metallic mix to the flake color chip I made. I take the KK01 and mix it in with some BC02 creating a red-toned metallic basecoat that comes very close to the flake color.

First of all, make a sample piece and use it to perfect your method. Then paint the vehicle. If I dream up a new way of applying flake, a few practice pieces will let me know if my idea will work before I mess up any parts.

The two biggest problems with painting flake colors are the rough surface of the freshly applied flake paint and the mess that results from the application. I have a few tricks I use to make the flake process fairly stress-free.

I'll address the last problem first. Flake is heavy stuff, heavier than metallics or pearl colors, and unless you're using a downdraft booth (a booth with the outtake filters right in the floor beneath the car) the flakes tend to land everywhere. The floor will be covered with them, and they'll try to get in every coat of paint you spray in the months after. So when planning out paint times, take into account the time it will take to clean up the excess flake. You can try and spray flake outside, where the flakes will land on the ground and stay out of your booth. However, the weather and zoning laws don't always cooperate with that. Besides, there will still be a mess of flake all over the ground for someone to deal with.

If you're attempting to spray flake in a garage, go out and get some disposable drop cloths. Drape them over everything, toolboxes, benches, everything. In fact, no matter what you choose to spray in your garage, cover everything with drop cloths. But remember: Never spray paint in a garage that is attached to your home, especially if the garage is located under the house.

To clean up flake, first I grab the shop vacuum and run it over the floor and any cobwebs that might have gathered in the corners. Then I sweep with a soft bristle broom, carefully looking to see how much flake is still there. The next step is mopping the floor, again looking to see how much

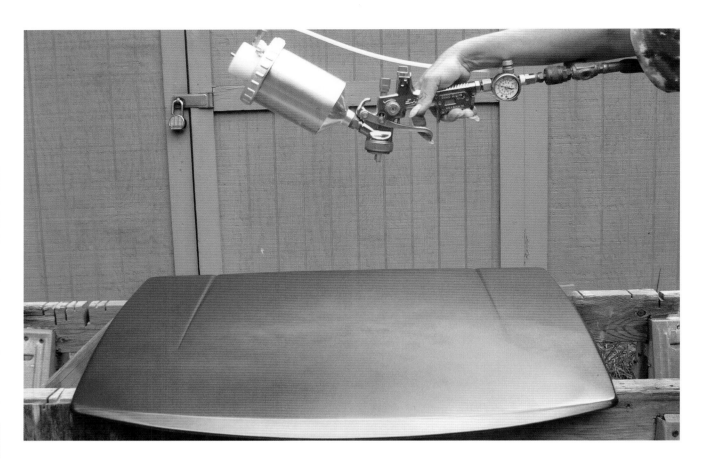

Here I spray two to three coats of the color-tone metallic. The biggest challenge to applying flake is obtaining good coverage. The more layers of flake applied, the rougher the surface will be and the more coats of clear will be necessary to smooth it out. Too many clear coats is not a good thing. So by using the metallic base under the flake coats, it won't take as much flake to cover the surface. Those spaces between the flakes won't be noticeable. HOK recommends not using more than three coats of flake. More than three coats will require tons of clear coating. Two to three coats of the metallic base coat are applied over the black base.

Next, mix up the flake. To spray F20 flake, HOK recommends mixing two level teaspoons (1ounce) of flake per quart of mixed clear coat. HOK makes a neat little adjustable spoon to precisely measure out the amount of flake you need. You can use most any kind of clear with your flake. In this instance I used HOK SG-100 Intercoat Clear mixed 2:1 with reducer. But I'm going to try something a little different here. I want to get a purple tone to this red flake base. So I mix just a little KK03 Wild Cherry into the mixed flake. Wild Cherry has a strong purple tone to it, but is still red.

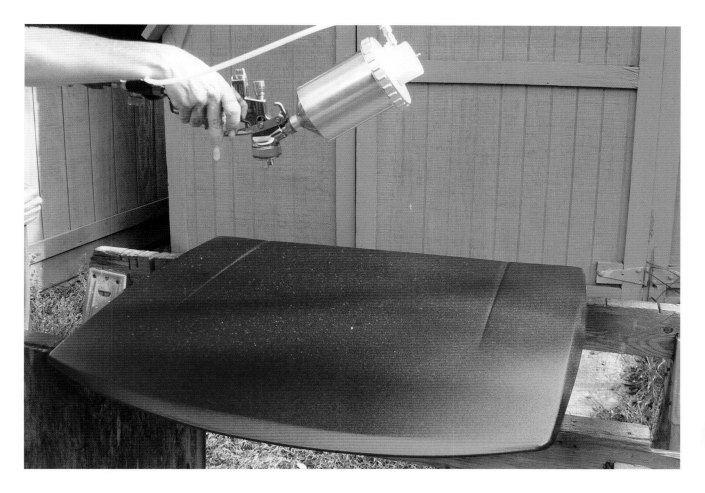

Now for the fun part: spraying the flake. Using the right tool for flake painting will make all the difference. Some painters use special flake guns, others drill out the nozzle on a junk gun. Flake will easily clog a spray gun and it takes practice to get a full, even coat of flake. I'm spraying at about 40 pounds of pressure.

flake remains. OK, now that you know how to clean up flake, let's talk about how to spray it.

Check to make sure there is flake coming out of the gun. Now adjust the gun and lay down the first coat of flake using a 50 percent pattern overlap. Hold the gun about six inches from the surface of the part. Any farther and the surface will be rough. Large flat topside areas like hoods and trunk lids will be the hardest to flake properly, as the flake will tend to be rough. Excess flake will land on wet areas and the edges will stick up. So spray the flake as flat as possible without it being too wet. This is one of those cases where it is really helpful to try out your technique on a spare hood. It's big and flat and will be a pain to apply flake to, so it's perfect for learning to spray flake. Three coats of flake work just fine, but for a truly wild flake layer you may want to play with trying four or five coats. Spray the flakes close to the surface, trying to lay them flat to reflect more light. Check the surface before applying each coat. See if it is getting a rough, hairy feel. Take a break before each coat to let

HANDY HINT

I used a SATA 2000 HVLP spray gun with the WSB nozzle set and a SATA Agitator mixing cup. A hose runs from the gun regulator to a quick-disconnect fitting on the lid of the cup. The lid has a paddle that reaches down into the cup and uses air to propel it and keep the flake mixed. With gravity-feed guns, the flake has a tendency to settle in the gun's paint chamber. If you suspect this is happening, hold a bundled rag over the gun nozzle and pull the trigger. It will force air through the paint chamber and into the cup, clearing out any clogging flakes. This trick can be used to keep the flake mixed in the cup, if an agitator cup is not used. Just give it a zap before applying each coat. But be sure not to blow the lid off the gun if it's a snap-on lid.

the last one dry. Your head will be clearer and the surface dry enough to touch, so you can actually feel it to see just how rough it is. Use common sense as you go.

If it is not too rough after your last flake coat, step back and dust a dry coat on, standing a few flakes up. *Do not overdo this step.*

There are two ways to proceed. If no further color is desired, you can go right to the clear coat process. But here candy color is applied over the flake. Mix up some clear (either urethane or base coat) and mix in candy concentrate or dye. I used the HOK KK-03 Wild Cherry. I mix up the color-toned clear, with not very much color for the first two coats. I like to layer it on very evenly. Then I put in more toner and get a "darker" clear color. In this example I put on four coats of candy. Next, it's time to hit the existing layers with your favorite filling clear. Three or four coats if you did not use any candy over your flake, two coats if you did.

There are those who recommend going straight to the clear color process and leaving the candy color application for a later time. In that procedure, apply the flake layers then apply three or four coats of clear urethane.

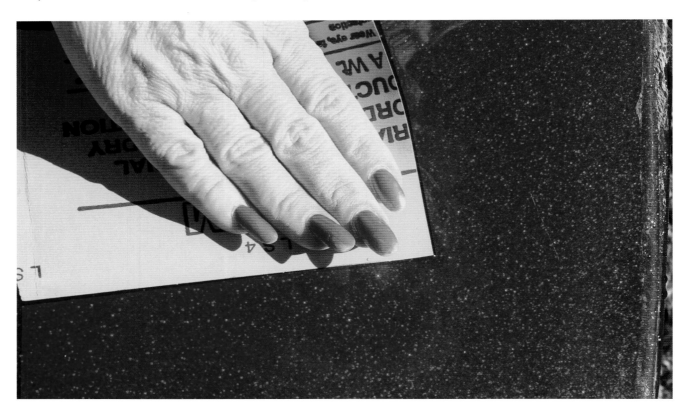

Wet sand with 600-grit, being careful not to sand too much and break through any flakes or the flake layers. If you get any light spots in candy flake jobs, retouch carefully with candy using an airbrush. Either way, once you've got the flake and/or color coats under the first round of clear, it should only require one more round of three or four clear coats and you're good to go. Now artwork or finishing clear coat can be applied. Depending on the amount of paint applied, it can take up to 30 days for the paint to dry enough for the flakes not to poke through the finish, as the clear dries around them.

Here's a close-up of the flake with candy over it. There will be artwork going over this base. The flake base paint really makes the paint job pop. The little white spots are the sunlight hitting the flakes.

Flake painting should be done on a sunny day in order to check the color and effect. Direct sunlight really brings out the true color and intensity of the flake.

37

CHAPTER 4
MARBLIZED BASE COAT PAINTING AND COLOR FADES

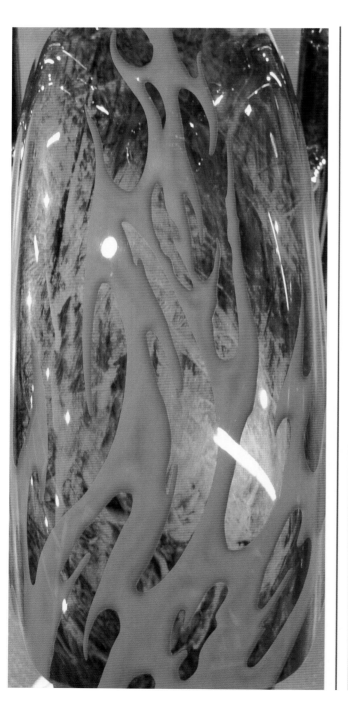

Everyone who has seen the paint in this picture asks me how I did it. Very simple: I broke the rules for painting marblizer. Marblizer isn't supposed to work if used like I used it. And it's certainly not supposed to last. I painted this bike for Sturgis 2002. Four years and many miles later, it still looks great.

It was absolute hell figuring out how to make this method work. And the first few tries failed miserably. It bubbled and lifted all over, and the candy separated from the marblizer base paint. The thing that mystified me was that the test piece had been a total success. I could have let tape sit on that part for a week and it wouldn't have lifted that paint when removed.

Then I realized the problem. I always abuse my test pieces, flooding on layers of paint, trying to make it screw up. After the paint bubbled for the second time, I ended up peeling all the parts with razor blades, sanding down what was left, and repriming everything in less than 24 hours. I was pretty sure I had the problem figured out. The next few days saw everything go from black to marblizer to urethane candy tangerine and into artwork. It was hell.

MATERIAL AND EQUIPMENT
House of Kolor MB-01 Silverwhite Marblizer
House of Kolor MB-00 Neutral Marblizer
Black basecoat
Any color candy paint (if applicable.)
Basecoat or Urethane clear
House of Kolor Intercoat Clear SG-100
Shiny masking paper
Masking tape
Gerson Blend Prep Tack Cloths
E-Z Mix cups
Plastic wrap or any odd non-cloth material
2 SATAjet 2000 Digital Spray Guns or
2 SATAminijet 4s, 1.2 nozzles (One spray gun is used to marblizing application, the other for black, candy, and clear coats)

The problem was (and all the folks who use basecoat clear for everything but final clear, are laughing at me right now) that the candy urethane coats were not bonding to the marblizing. On the two failed attempts, I had laid down a few coats of Intercoat Clear, but for fear of blurring the marblizer I had not applied them heavy enough to bond everything together. I had hammered that Intercoat on the sample piece. It was a hard lesson, but I learned a lot.

In the following step-by-step I explain several ways of applying marblizer. My infamous marblizing technique described previously is last. Some other painters may do it differently, but this is how I do it. If it doesn't work for you and it peels or bubbles, just keep trying. But try it first on a test part. Remember, this is not the approved way to apply marblizer.

It's a matter of personal preference, but when it comes to cars and trucks marblizing is not usually effective for overall base coat painting. It is best used for artwork like flames and graphics. Some use it as a deepening or shadowing effect behind flames or graphics. It also works well for two-tone paint. Another slick idea is to paint a car black, and then fade in marblizer on the top or bottom half, using thinned-down black to soften the transition. Total marblizing is a very busy effect to put over an entire car. The step-by-step presented in this chapter was done on a Mini hood I was painting for SATA spray equipment to be displayed at the 2005 International Autobody Congress & Exhibition.

EASY ONE-LAYER MARBLIZING

Get the car and/or parts in black. I use plastic wrap to manipulate the House of Kolor Marblizer. Here I used silver. HOK makes a few different colors, and any one of them can be used. Tear off a sheet of plastic wrap and have it close by. The main thing about marblizing is that it dries very fast. It takes a few tries to get used to it. So have a plan of attack as to the areas that will be worked on. Apply the first layer of marblizer by doing one side of a part at a time, like the top of the fender above the body trim line then the bottom half of the fender, and so on. Spray a medium wet coat of marblizer.

Quickly grab the plastic wrap and stick it against the wet marblizer and move it around. Another tip—I keep the plastic sheet from getting flat. If I'm marblizing the top of a fender and want a long pattern on it, I'll have long folds or wrinkles in the plastic and lay it on like that, then move it, and the folds create long, dark streaks in the marblizer surface. Go over the surface, bit by bit. Now keep in mind if you desire a dark texture with lots of black showing through and vivid contrast between the black and marblizer, be careful when spraying the marblizer or the silver overspray will mute out that awesome pattern on the hood as you spray other areas of the car. Keep the gun pressure low, about 20 to 25 pounds. Now while I could use a regular size gun, I'll use a small spray gun, like the SATAminijet 4 seen here. This is because the hood I'm working on is small and I'll be only be working on one area at a time. The minijet puts out less pressure and keeps the marblizer in the area being worked on. Overspray can land on other parts of the panel and mute the darker dramatic areas of marblizer. For applying a marblized effect to taped-off graphics or flames, a mini gun works best. If fading in marblizing on whole surfaces, a regular spray gun should be used.

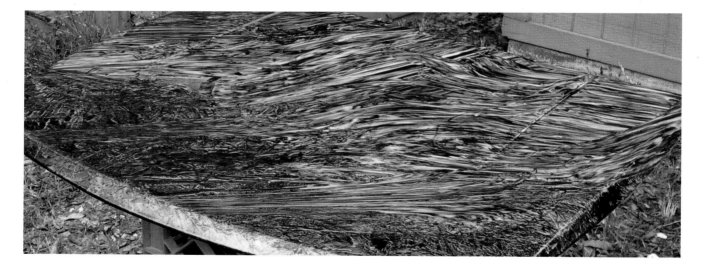

This is where you stop if you're going for minimal marblizing and lots of black. For a dark, dramatic effect, don't overmarblize. If you end up with too much marblizer and want to see more black or you want to create more black swirls or texture, get some House of Kolor Neutral Marblizer MB-00. Spray a wet layer of that on right where you want to make the change, slap a clean piece of plastic wrap on, and move it into the pattern you want. Remove the plastic and let the part dry. Wait 30 minutes and apply one or two medium coats of HOK Intercoat Clear thinned down 50 percent (2 to 1). This is critical! If this step is not done, delamination problems may occur. Candy top coats may now be applied. If using urethane top coats, wait 15 to 60 minutes before clearing. No wait is needed if using base coat clear.

MULTILAYER MARBLIZING

There are two ways the metal or foil effect can be done. One is to continue spraying on coats of marblizer and manipulating them with the plastic. The other is more risky, because the layers won't bond. The first process is easier but not as effective. Continue spraying on layers using the method gone through previously. Wait 15–20 minutes between coats. Go from area to area, using the Neutral Marblizer to redo areas that don't have enough black streaks showing or where it looks too even. Let the layers dry 30 minutes. Then apply two medium coats of House of Kolor SG-100 Intercoat Clear.

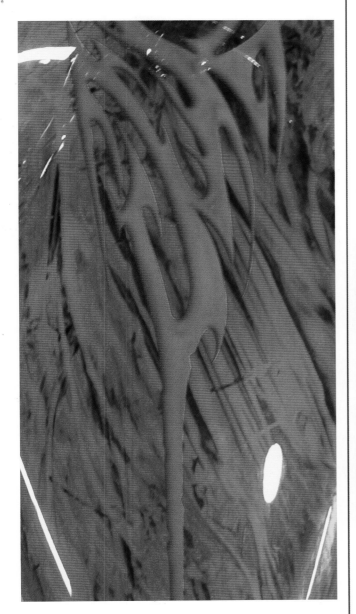

Note the long, dark streaks.

This is the trick. If sprayed on correctly, it will reach down through the layers of marblizer and bond them together. If sprayed too dry, it won't penetrate properly. If sprayed too heavy, the marblizer will soften too much and the dramatic effect will dissipate.

Wait 30 minutes and then apply three coats of urethane clear or go straight to candy coats using candy urethane or "uro," which is base coat or Intercoat clear mixed with candy concentrate.

THE KILLER MARBLIZING EFFECT

Now for the risky process, but the one that achieves the total foil effect seen at the left.

Please try this first on a test part. I can't even imagine trying to get this stuff off a whole car. Make sure the process works for you and doesn't lift or bubble. It may take a day or two for the bubbles to pop up, and the bubbles won't appear until after the urethane is applied. Even if only base coat clear is used, the bubbles may still be present.

After the sample is dry, test it to make sure the urethane top coat is sticking to the marblizer. This is done by sticking 2-inch masking tape on the dry painted surface and then pulling it up an hour later. Do everything you can to try and make that top coat come up.

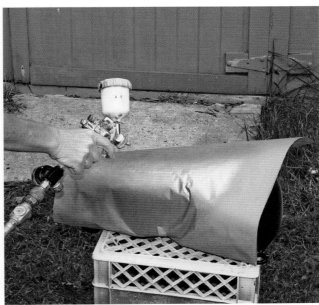

First Step: *Wrap high-quality or glossy masking paper around a spare or junk part. Do the first layer of marblizing on your parts. Now work on one major area of a panel at a time. I use the same piece of plastic for each area, moving the plastic when I move to the next area. Start by spraying a layer of marblizer on the masking paper.*

Slap the plastic wrap on it and "pick up" the marblizer on the plastic.

Quickly lay the plastic over the area being marblized and move it around. Repeat the process over and over until the desired effect is achieved. You must work fast, keeping the marblizer wet as it is transferred. It's easy to see how the process works after the first transfer. The amount of marblizer that is picked up and the way it is moved around will determine the pattern you get. I like to drag the plastic across the part, creating long streaks.

HANDY HINT

Watch for dry bits of marblizer getting trapped under layers. Check each part after layering on the material. Brush off raised, dry bits with your fingers. I've used as many as four layers of marblizer on one part, and it's important to keep things clean between layers.

Play around with the wrinkles in the plastic while picking up marblizer. Here I want long streaks.

Above left: *Then either stretch open the plastic or leave it wrinkled and apply it on the car or part.* **Above right:** *Once the desired effect is achieved, it's time for the most important step. Here I'm doing about four layers of marblizing using the transfer method. Clearing over these layers with the Intercoat Clear is critical with this process. Wait 30 minutes before applying it. In order for the layers to bond, the Intercoat must penetrate right down to the black. That was the mistake I made in my story. With the sample, I flooded on the Intercoat Clear nearly heavy enough to mottle the marblizer. I was more careful when working on the actual parts, and that was my mistake. After all the layers are done and the Intercoat is on, apply the desired candy or clear coats. Be sure to wait 30 minutes if using urethane for your topcoat.*

And that's it. Here is the finished result. I can't guarantee this will work perfectly for all painters. But it is how I do it. As always, while using any House of Kolor product, make sure you have their tech manual close by. I can't remember everything, so I find myself opening up that book more than I want to admit. Read Chapter 14 of this book for clearing info. If a few small isolated bubbles do come up, they can be dug out with a stencil knife, filled, and remarblized. If more than just a few raise up, sandblast or peel, but don't say I didn't warn you. But do try again on a test part. It is an awesome effect that can be successfully painted if done correctly. Read further for candy application.

COLOR FADES

Since this is a sample piece, I can play around with it. I decide to do a candy color fade from HOK KK02 Lime Gold to KK08 Tangerine. I mix the candy concentrates with urethane clear. They can also be mixed with base coat clear. Use whatever system you are familiar with. The reason I'm using urethane is that is flows out to a nice gloss, so I can clearly see the result as I'm spraying. Sometimes base coat can tend to look dry, and it has to be "rewetted" to see the detail.

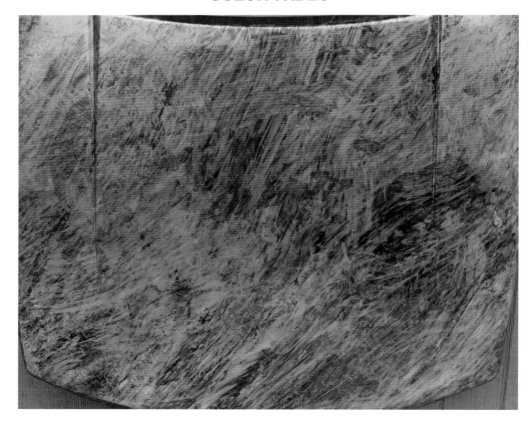

Gun technique, as well as paint mixture, is what will make a good color fade. This is the gun position I start the fade with, gun pointing straight down at the surface. I'm using a SATA 2000 HVLP. Note how I am holding the hose with my free hand to keep it away from the hood. Note those overalls—pretty cute huh? Very important: Use a tack rag after each coat of paint when doing fades! On this hood I tack ragged the yellow area after each coat, staying away from the tangerine, as it was sticky with fresh urethane. Overspray from other colors will extend the fade much farther than planned and can ruin the fade. In this case, if I had not tacked it, the whole hood would have been orange.

HANDY HINT

When mixing paint to be used to color fades, always mix it thinner than usual. For solid colors, reduce them down. For candy colors, use candy concentrates mixed with clear and keep the candy on the thin side. You want the fade to be gradual and the paint needs to have an almost transparent look to it. If the paint is thick, the fade will have a grainy look to it. You'll be able to actually see the individual grains of paint on the surface. I reduce my paint as much as possible to get a very, very fine grain of paint spray. Using the proper gun also helps. Using an HVLP spray gun will break down the paint more than a regular pressure gun. Before trying any color fade, try out the mixtures on a test panel. Then look closely. Can the actual grains of paint be seen? If so, the mix is too thick. Reduce and try again. Remember, it is better to go too light than too dark. You can always go back and add more coats. For solid color base coat fades, you can also mix in reduced base coat clear to help reduce the amount of color in the mix.

When the gun reaches the fade area, I arc it up and reduce the pressure on the trigger so I'm spraying less paint. This is what first time "faders" need to practice, coordinating the flip and the trigger action. Note the position of the gun above the hood. See how much farther the tangerine extends past the gun? That's how far the paint will travel. This is why care must be taken when spraying fades, as the color always travels farther than expected.

I'm using HOK's UC-35 urethane clear. I'll mix in some Lime Gold candy concentrate, about four parts clear to one part concentrate. Using a SATA 2000, I spray two coats on the bottom half of the hood. Now I could have covered the hood, but I decide not to. Next I mix up some urethane with the tangerine concentrate. This is where it gets tricky.

I start the tangerine application at the top of the hood. Overspray will want to travel down into the yellow, so for the first coat only spray half as far as you want the orange to be. This picture shows how the hood looked after the first coat of orange. Note the area where the two colors meet. This is the fade and no orange will be directly applied here.

I continue spraying tangerine, keeping the passes of the spray gun toward the top of the hood, covering less area with each pass until only the top edge receives paint. Here is the finished hood the next morning.

HANDY HINT

Here is the finished hood on the cloudy day it was painted. Compare that to the previous photo taken on a sunny morning. Note the difference? Light truly affects the way colors appear. This is why painters need to check custom colors in all types of light.

CHAPTER 5
AIRBRUSHES AND OTHER FORMS OF TORTURE

THE ESSENTIAL EQUIPMENT

Years ago I knew the location, quality of copies, and hours of every copy machine within a 30-minute drive from my home. I'd break the speed of sound trying to get to one with great enlargement and reduction capabilities before they closed. There were times when it felt like my life depended on it. Copy machines saved me hours of resizing drawings by hand. They took all guesswork out of it. Then someone invented personal computers with scanners and printers, and suddenly instead of stressing at the wheel I could stay at home and get a whole lot more work done. If you don't have a computer, most drug stores and many other places have copiers that will reduce and enlarge drawings or photos.

I keep the drawing board close by for tracing the reverse side of drawings or to draw out stuff. I also tape a piece of thin cardboard on one side of the drawing board and cut out all my stencils on that. They seem to cut better against a soft surface. Plus, after the cardboard surface gets all marred by the cuts, I just tape on a new one. It saves the wooden cutting board and makes for quick and easy stencil cutting. I also use a cutting plotter sometimes. But I find for most of my applications, it's just quicker and easier to cut out my stencils by hand.

Cars, trucks, and boats are large surfaces to work on. One piece of essential time-saving equipment is a projector. The top panel flips up to reveal a glass surface. Simply place the drawing or photo you are working from face down on the glass plate. Then place the projector the necessary distance from the surface being worked on. The farther away the projector is, the larger the image will appear. The lens tube slides back and forth to focus the image. Once the image is displayed on the desired surface, just draw it on the prepped surface with a lead pencil or Stabilo pencil. Then you're ready to airbrush. But one factor to consider is that the brighter the light in the shop, the less visible the image projected will be. Just like any other tool, the more a projector is used, the more effective the artist will become with it. I use an Artograph Super Prism projector. They run about $200.

Taking a break from flaming two hot rods.

Here the image of a grim reaper is projected onto a hood. The room is nearly dark and the hood is white, while the reaper is a black outline. Yet, it is not as visible as you would think. Projectors are great, but they do have their limitations.

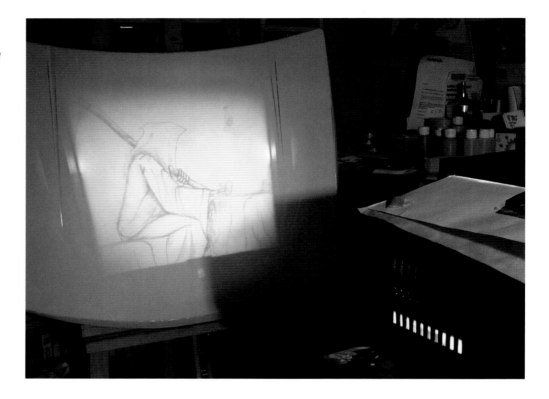

A light box is also an essential piece of my equipment. You can buy them online for as little as $55. Don't have a light box? You can make one using a plastic crate, a sheet of clear Plexiglas and a light bulb fixture. Or just tape whatever you're tracing to a window (during the day, of course) and trace away.

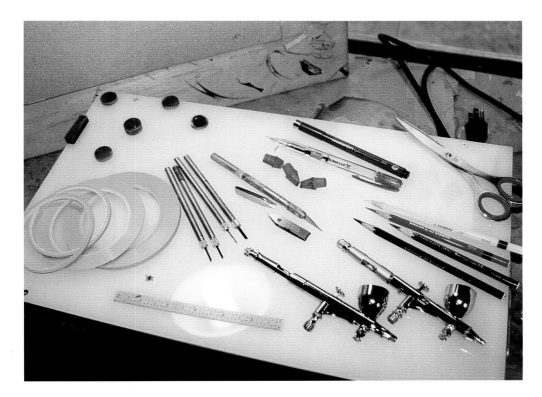

Other airbrushing tools I cannot live without (clockwise from upper left): drawing board, magnets, pink erasers, mechanical pencil, fineline permanent marker, high-quality scissors, Stabilo pencils, Iwata airbrushes, X-Acto Number 11 knife, Uncle Bill's Sliver Gripper tweezers (available online for $6.85 at www.magellans.com), X-Acto Number 4 stencil knives, 3M green fineline tape. Also, my television.

Magnets hold paper stencils in place on metal surfaces. Pink erasers, like the pointed ones that go on the end of a pencil, come in very handy. They're not just for erasing pencil lines and rubbing off frisket adhesive from painted surfaces; they also can be used to erase overspray that creeps in between pieces of tape. I just finished touching up a logo on a tank and some overspray had sneaked between bits of masking tape. Under the rework, there was plenty of clear, so the overspray rubbed right off without affecting the original artwork. Mechanical pencils are great for getting the very fine lines needed on stencils and such. Fineline permanent markers are often used in artwork to get superfine detail. I use a selection of scissors to cut out paper stencils. Stabilo pencils are great when working on fine details, like faces, and you can clear coat over them. I know artists who have done entire murals using only Stabilos. I use the tweezers to grab frisket when removing it and to handle tiny tape ends. It's easier than trying to maneuver and place them with my fingers. I prefer the small Number 4 knives to any others when cutting frisket paper, and they are small enough to maneuver around curves, but Number 11 knives work better for cutting paper stencils. I use a smooth white cutting stone to keep the blades sharp. Some painters will only use blue fineline tape as they feels it hugs the curves better than the green, but I like the green fineline. I feel it lays down a straighter line than the blue because it is stiffer. It comes in many different widths, and the 1/16-inch tape holds a sharp curve if firmly pressed down and then taped around the unpainted side of the curve, especially if masking tape is run alongside the sharp curves. You may need to go back and burnish down the curves just before you spray paint.

HANDY HINT

Airbrushing can be stressful and tedious. I find having a TV or music on gives background noise and takes the edge off the atmosphere. Also, it can add to the mood. If I'm working on a medieval themed mural, I'll put a barbarian movie on and find it helps my frame of mind. Some people prefer music. The point is to make your painting atmosphere as pleasant and relaxing as possible. It can be very distracting doing artwork in a body shop. Everyone wants to stop and watch. And this is always when things go wrong. Some artists thrive on being watched, but it took me some getting used to. Yet there are times when it is very handy to have opinions. It's easy to focus so hard on a project that essential flawed elements are missed. For example, a design could be slightly slanted, or maybe the design is off balanced, or the symmetry is off. And the only way to really see it is to stand back for while and just look at it with fresh eyes. I take regular breaks from working and stand back to study the car, checking out the progress of the artwork.

For stencils, I prefer Grafix brand frisket paper, GerberMask (a low-tack vinyl stencil film), and MetalFlake Corporation Spray Mask (1-800-227-2683). Many airbrush artists successfully use transfer tape as stencil material. Sticky Mickey transfer tape (1-800-423-3071) was developed by artist Mickey Harris, especially for use as stencil material. But there are times when I need to see the background artwork through the mask, and most transfer tape is opaque. TransferRite Ultra Transfer Tape is clear, and I find I'm using it more and more. I also keep a soft measuring tape handy for referencing around fenders and trunk lids. And I keep 6-inch, 15-inch, and 36-inch steel rulers around, as well as a steel measuring tape.

Flexible drafting templates, like circles, ellipses, and ovals, and specialized airbrushing stencils, like Craig Fraser's line of skull stencils are things I also use quite a bit. Artool makes all kinds of great freehand shields, with shapes that can be used for almost anything. You can find these stencils at most online art stores.

FINDING MATERIALS AND EQUIPMENT

Most paint, sandpaper, and taping materials can be found at automotive paint supply stores. Transfer tape and Gerber paint masks are found at sign supply stores. Different stores carry different lines of paint, like PPG, DuPont, etc. But most stores carry House of Kolor, which can also be found at online paint stores. Call the store first to find out if they carry the line or brand of paint you want. Artist tools and materials can be found at art supply stores. I buy most of my stuff online. Sites like bear-air.com, coastairbrush.com, dixieart.com, dickblick.com, and misterart.com are some of the places I find everything from airbrushes to Stabilo pencils. If you have difficulty finding a product, just go online and use a search website.

HIGH TECH

These days, computer equipment is a bargain. A desktop computer paired with a scanner and printer can be found for $500 or less.

SETTING UP YOUR WORKSPACE

Try to have the car in a place where it can stay until the artwork is completed. You'll be spending many hours airbrushing, so make it as comfortable as possible. I find that rolling mechanic's stools work great. Plus most have a handy storage space to keep tools in easy reach. For working down low on vehicles, I lay a large beach towel, sheet,

HANDY HINT

For items like hoods, trunk lids, or other removable parts, I use an artist's easel to hold the part. In some cases, when the parts are very heavy, panel holders can be used or you can even make a super heavy duty easel out of wood.

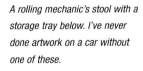

A rolling mechanic's stool with a storage tray below. I've never done artwork on a car without one of these.

or big piece of cardboard down next to the car. You'll want to sit up as straight as possible. Don't let your back hunch or slump, because you'll be in serious pain the next day, or even in a few hours.

Keep everything handy and within easy reach. Paint bottles can get out of control. Try not to have more colors mixed than being used on any particular job. But always have white, black, and other commonly used colors mixed up and ready to spray. After a job is finished, try to go through the work area and put all paperwork related to that job in a file. Then clean up the area. Hours can be wasted trying to find stuff. Take the time to have a system. It's great to be working on an eagle and be able to quickly pull up a drawing or photograph to reference, or leftover feather stencils to help with a new eagle mural. Each paint job I do gets a file.

Try to have the car or truck near an overhead door. There will be times when it's very helpful to roll the car outside to check artwork or colors in the sunlight. Plus, it makes for easier wet sanding as the water doesn't get all over the shop floor.

LIGHTING

Depending on the shop or space you are doing the artwork in, chances are additional lighting will be needed. Ideally, you would think a professional paint booth, with its great

lighting, would work best for artwork. But I find that the close quarters of a spray booth make it difficult to step back and plan out my artwork, gauge how effective it is, or if I even like the way it is turning out. I like to work where I can stand back and spend time contemplating the overall design or how effective it is. Cars need to be viewed from farther away than the 3 or 4 feet of extra space a spray booth provides. I usually keep the vehicle close to an overhead door with plenty of space on both sides. But ventilation can be a problem. The shop I paint in has an area with overhead doors and two connecting walls. If I'm doing a lot of artwork spraying, I'll open both doors halfway even if it is cold. You have to get that overspray out.

If I will be doing a lot of heavy spraying, I'll lay out the artwork or apply masks out in the shop just beyond the spray booth, then roll the car into the booth for the actual paint application.

An open garage door can let in all kinds of natural light, but with weather extremes that is not always possible. I'll use small halogen shop lights to throw more light where I need it. I always try to position the car where it can get as much natural light as possible. Many times, I'll even roll the car outside the shop to check the artwork in the sun.

I've used portable lights outdoors, indoors, anywhere I'm doing artwork. I love working outdoors because the light is great. But that seldom is possible. Check out Chapters 6 and 7. I painted those cars in my favorite place to work on car. There are overhead doors with windows on two sides and plenty of room to stand back. The spray booth is located just forward of this area. I can roll the car into it if necessary. Plus, there are even two skylights in the roof to let in natural light. But many times I still find I need more light. That's where portable lights come in. I usually use two lights shining on the artwork area. One light on one side, another light on the other. This way they cancel out the shadows each one is throwing.

AIRBRUSHES

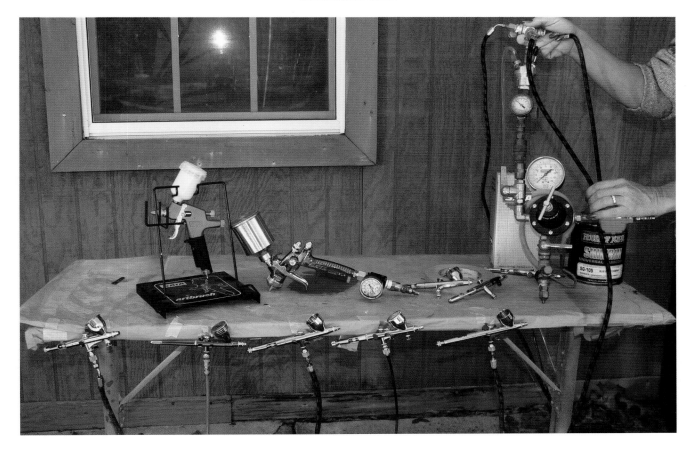

I like using a full-size spray regulator as it keeps the air pressure nice and constant. This was a jury-rigged setup that somehow I've never taken the time to update. I just keep adding more fittings and hoses. I can quickly break it down from my shop set up, load it into a bag, and set it up on location anywhere. I use a homemade air manifold made out of pipefittings. There are commercial manifolds on the market, but these tend to be pricey. A little common sense goes a long way. At some discount stores you can find aluminum blocks with quick-disconnect fittings already installed. Go to most quality auto parts or hardware stores, and go through their air hose or pipes fitting trays. Take along the fittings for your airbrush hoses and design your own set up. I mount the regulator on the side of a table or rollaround tool cart and tape airbrush holders on the edge of the table or cart. There's plenty of space for my airbrush bottles.

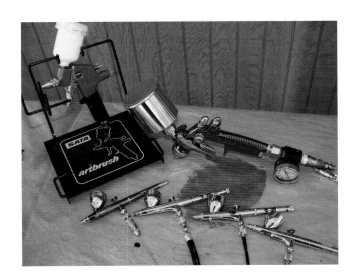

I have six airbrushes in my shop. Most artists have a favorite kind of airbrush. I used Badger 150 siphon-feed or bottle-feed airbrushes for years and got great results with them. The range of needles and tips allowed me to go from fine hairlines to wide spray. And the price was right. Then in the mid 1990s I switched over to gravity- or top-feed airbrushes for greater control of fine detail. I use a SATAgraph 3 and 1 top-feed for most of my detail work. I also use Iwata HP-Cs and Micron C airbrushes. With gravity-feed brushes, I like the way I can remove the crown cap/spray regulator and get a very fine line for details, then put it back on for shading and fades. For larger spray needs, I use a SATA dekor 2000 artbrush and a SATAminijet 4. The SATA artbrush has a wide range of nozzle sizes from 0.2 to 1.0 millimeter. For beginner airbrushers, the top feed Iwata Eclipse is a good choice. I use them a lot.

HANDY HINT

One thing I love about the SATA artwork system is the quick disconnect hoses. You can quickly switch from the Dekor artbrush to the SATAgraph airbrush.

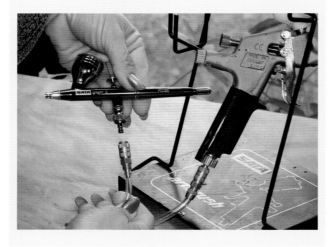

AIRBRUSH MAINTENANCE

All kinds of things can go wrong with airbrushes, but dried paint clogging the nozzle is the biggest problem. Know your airbrush. Learn how to take it apart and thoroughly clean it with lacquer thinner. I remove the needle and use good quality cotton swabs to clean out the color cup on my gravity-feed airbrushes. Little round bristle brushes can also be used to clean out passages. See Chapter 15 for more info.

PAINT FOR AIRBRUSHING

Lacquer atomizes down finer than any other kind of automotive paint. Some airbrushers refuse to use any other paint. I switched over to uncatylized base coat enamels 10 years ago, and it took some getting used to. I currently use House of Kolor for much of my art.

Many painters believe the future of paint is water-based paint. Water-base has come a long, long way. Many airbrush artists are enjoying the new Auto Air line of water-based paint. I don't have enough experience to talk much about it, but like any paint, the more you use it the better you'll be. Like it or not, it is the future and the sooner a painter starts using it, the more experience is gained, the better that product will work for the painter.

More and more painters are using Auto Air, and their range of colors is quite extensive and getting more extreme every day. Some of their colors are very exciting, but like any paint, I like getting used to it before I use it on customers' jobs. Other companies are also developing water-based paint, so these products will only keep improving.

Every type and brand of paint has its own qualities that the airbrusher has to become familiar with. Some painters like Brand X and some swear by Brand Y. The best thing to do is try out a type and brand of paint by buying a pint of black, a pint of white, and some reducer. Then play around with it. Get used to it. Is it too grainy, or does it make the airbrush spit no matter how much it is reduced down? Try another brand. I have seen all kinds of awesome mural work, and when I ask what brand of paint the artist used I get a different answer each time.

The brand of paint I use is House of Kolor. I have had very good results, and it has proved to be very, very, durable, dependable, and easy to work with—if used properly. I keep my airbrush paint mixtures in plastic bottles with caps on them, and I agitate them often while working. I find these at coastairbrush.com.

Back in the days before gravity feed guns, most painters simply mixed their paint right in the cup. Not a good idea, but we still did it. These disposable mixing cups from E-Z Mix are great. They're economical, they come in different sizes, and they have a variety of various measurements on them that make it easy to mix up paint, whether it's 3-2-1 or 4-1-1 or 1-1. Remember to always strain your paint.

As for design colors, like pearls and specialty colors for graphics and flames, I truly recommend House of Kolor. There are some artwork results that would only be possible by using HOK. Their Shimrin pearls dry quickly, cover great with minimal coats, and work very well with other brands of paint. I keep an inventory of these pearls and find I keep using them. Some painters have their own mixing systems and can mix up pearls of the specific paint brand they use, but many of them still use HOK Designer Pearls. And for the painter who doesn't have a mixing system, keeping a small inventory of HOK will come in extremely handy.

Other paint companies are also coming out with more specialty paints, and I look forward to having some fun with those. Having more paint companies with custom paint lines means more choices for the custom painter.

SAFETY

One thing that is very essential while airbrushing is proper ventilation. If I'm not in a spray booth, I have a small fan off to the side behind me pushing fresh air past my face, and I wear a respirator. As I've said previously, I like working as close to an outside door as possible, and I like getting the paint fumes out of my work space as quickly as possible. During the day I love the natural light that comes in the windows in the door, but you don't want to work with the sun hitting you in the face. I've had work areas that were in shops with no windows, surrounded by concrete and equipment. It definitely had a negative effect on my work. I find that I do my best work near an open door.

Folks ask me how I can do such tedious work for hours on end. Over the years I've learned what works for me, what gets me the best results in my artwork. Calm, quiet, peaceful surroundings with no distractions work for me. Other artists thrive in shops that put them in contact with people. Find what works for you and what kind of atmosphere you feel happy and relaxed in.

Other safety considerations with airbrushing are paint storage, ventilation, and cleanup. I keep very little paint on my work cart, only the colors for the artwork I am doing that day. All other paint is stored in a climate-controlled shed that is not attached to my home or shop. More paint cans sitting around mean more fumes.

When I clean my guns or airbrushes I always wear vinyl gloves. If I can possibly help it, lacquer thinner never touches my hands. Solvents absorb through the skin very quickly and can have the same effect as if you had breathed them in. Always use common sense. But if you're breathing fumes, your thinking will get fuzzy and common sense will go out the window.

REFERENCE LIBRARY AND IDEAS

I've talked about this in other chapters, but it's worth mentioning here. Build a good photo reference library. If you plan on painting realistic murals of wolves or eagles, a $25 investment in a book on wildlife is money well spent, as that book will give you ideas and great photos to work from for years. I have 25 years of books and reference materials in my library. I can find a photo of nearly anything I need

My reference library.

FABRICATION PHOTOS

When dealing with any vehicle, get photos of the car or truck. That way you'll see how the parts sit on the vehicle. Many times much of the vehicle may be taped off during the artwork phase and these photos will come in handy. You may need to know how the fender lines up with the hood or what will be covered by bumpers and other accessories. Plus, it can be essential when figuring out the artwork design. Having photos to look at before doing the job will aid in coming up with ideas. Make copies of the photos and play around by drawing out ideas on the copies.

PREPAINT DRAWINGS

As is discussed in some of the chapters, I often do drawings before I do artwork. This way I can visualize, plan, and fine-tune my work before I even touch the sheet metal. I use a combination of my reference library, a computer with Photoshop, a light box, and drawing by hand to arrange and think out the drawings. This is where photos of the vehicle are essential.

A simple trick: Take the photo of the car being painted and make an enlarged copy of it. Then, with whiteout, paint out the stuff that will be painted, like side panels, roof, trunk, etc. Now make a few copies of that. Or place an enlarged copy of the picture on a light box or taped to a window. Put tracing paper over it and trace the outlines of the car and its parts. Make a few copies of that. Now you have plenty of "blanks" of the car to play around with. The finished drawings can be submitted to the customer who can approve or advise in making changes. Chapter 6 will show how I (very crudely) design a paint job using Photoshop.

In addition to base coat samples, many times I also test my artwork colors and techniques on spare or junk panels or sign blanks. Countless hours can be saved. Plus the customer can also approve the test part and drawings. The painter's sanity can be saved, because the customer can't later claim dissatisfaction with the design and/or colors.

to airbrush. And what's not there is most likely on my computer, where I have many photos and pieces of artwork loaded on my hard drive.

There are so many places to go for inspiration. I always pick up sport truck magazines and look for paint that catches my eye. It can be the combination of colors used in a particular paint job or the design itself. Sometimes an idea just pops into my head. Then I find the photos that help me develop that idea. Other times I have to go through my reference material to get ideas. Maybe I'll see a graphic with a small detail I want to use. I'll save that and change it around.

Save as many photos and ideas as possible, but make sure to have a system in place to organize them all. I even have a box filled with photos filed in envelopes with headings such as "wolves," "women," "backgrounds," etc.

A few prepaint drawings.

MAKING SIDES MATCH

Here's how I used this technique on the Camaro. On paper, I've drawn a flame design using a picture of the old car and enlarged it to the size it needs to be on the new car. A projector could have also been used, but the light in the shop was too bright and other painters were working in the shop. Refer to chapters 8, 9, and 10 for detailed photos of other examples.

Using a pencil, I trace along the lines of the design. If the design is to be repeated, flip it over and place the tracing paper on a light table or window. Now the lines will show through the paper. Trace along the lines with a pencil, flip it over, and it is ready to be placed on the surface to be painted.

Now, I would have loved to show more of this project, but shortly after these pictures were taken, it turned into a

The subject here is a lovely 1970 Camaro. The owner wants to duplicate a flame paint job that was on a car he owned in high school. The flames will branch off the yellow/orange strip already painted on the car.

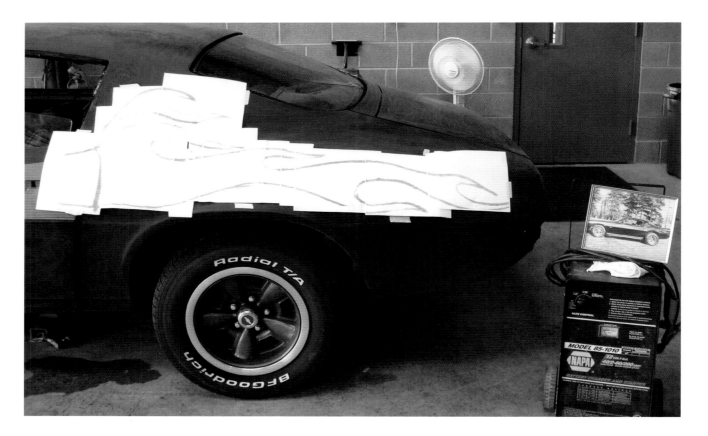

This method of making sides match can apply to opposite sides of a car or whenever a design needs to be repeated or reversed. Once the design is laid out and taped off or cut out on one side of the part, tape a piece of tracing or masking paper over it. Then, using a pencil, simply trace along the tape edge. Then flip it over, tape it to a window during the day, and trace the lines on the backside of the drawing as they will be visible through the paper. Then flip it over, take reference measurements from the first side for the car, line up the drawing, and trace along the lines. A pencil line image will be transferred to the surface of the car. In the lower right corner the original photo of the original car can be seen.

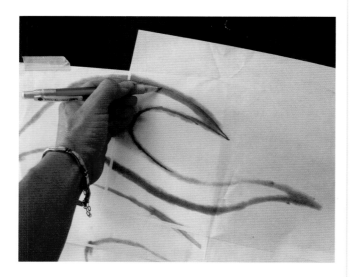

Then trace along the lines. It will leave an imprint of the design on the surface. The flame design will now be visible once the paper is removed.

nightmare and I needed to be kept away from anything I could throw, like expensive cameras. This is a harsh reality of custom painting. Projects can and do turn into nightmares. Sometimes it's the paint or the equipment. Or the planned artwork doesn't work. And sometimes customers should not come within 100 miles of the paint shop while the project is being worked on.

ARTWORK MATCHING AND REVERSING: ANOTHER TRICK

Another trick in getting sides to match is to do the artwork on one side of the car or truck. Then, once it's done, take a digital picture of it. Load the photo into your computer, reverse it with a graphics program, and print it out. For murals, try to resize it so it's the same size as the actual artwork. Tape it to the surface near the artwork or have it close by. It makes doing reversed artwork a whole lot easier. Paper stencils can also be made from any copies of the reversed photo.

The flame design is taped off with 1/8-inch green fineline tape. Now I see the design needs to be altered so that high point on the lower side of the design is centered over the wheelwell. The tape is left in place and new tape is run along where the lines will be. Then the parts of the old tape that aren't needed are cut away.

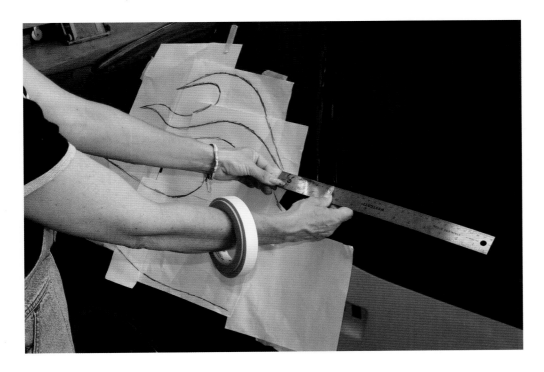

Now, to reverse the design for use on the opposite side of the car, simply flip it over. The pencil lines are already there. And the lines on the side against the surface of the car are covered with pencil from tracing them on the first side. So all I have to do is line up the drawing and trace along those lines. I take measurements from the first side to get reference points to aid in lining up the design on the other side.

59

HANDY HINT

Clear coat changes everything. It can be very hard to see just how effective your artwork will be until it is clear coated. Layers of artwork can tend to appear very two-dimensional as they are being worked on. As clear coat is layered over, the layers appear to separate and the three-dimensional effect can come to life. In order to see how effective the artwork is as it is being worked on, some artists will wipe over the surface with a gentle postpainting cleaner like HOK's KC-20. Do not use hard pressure when wiping, just gently wash over the surface with the cleaner on a cloth. If it is applied too heavily or rubbed too hard, some of the artwork may come off, especially if the thin layers of white details are airbrushed.

If I'm airbrushing very thin layers of color, such as subtle shading on skin tones or hair, I'll take care not to disturb it in any way. Unless of course I've touched it and left an oily fingerprint that needs to be removed.

REWORKING ARTWORK

I tend to do my rework after the first coats of clear are applied. If my first artwork attempt isn't perfect, I don't sweat it. I save my artwork under clear coat. Then I look it over, seeing where I need to make changes. Many times I take a clipboard with either a digital photo or drawing of the parts and mark on the photo or drawing where I need to do rework. This is especially helpful when touching up graphics and flames. Those little lines aren't always perfect on the first try. Don't freak over artwork mistakes. Most of the time it can be fixed with rework. Even the very best painters have to go back and fix stuff.

MISCELLANEOUS DESIGN LAYOUT HINTS

Say you need to move a stencil or cutout. You have it all taped on. But it needs to be moved ¼ inch to the left. Lay out fineline tape all around the stencil except on the side in the direction it needs to be moved. Now lay a line of tape ¼ inch from the edge of the stencil. Now the stencil can be carefully peeled up and put exactly where it needs to go, because there's a location reference for three sides.

After I draw out designs on spray mask or the surface of the part, I lay fineline tape along the lines and trace with a pen or pencil to help smooth out the lines.

Say there's fineline tape laying out a graphic along the side of a car and the line needs to be moved slightly. If I needed a line to be moved ¼ inch, I put down ¼ inch tape

along the original fineline tape in whatever direction the line needs to move in. Then simply tape off the newly put down tape.

When trying to come up with a design, there are times when it is best to sketch the design directly on the car. But you don't want to cover the cars with lots of confusing lines from different ideas. Wrap masking paper over the hood or whatever surface. For sketching out designs on curved surfaces like fenders, wrap it in masking paper, but cut slots in the paper and the paper will fold right around the curves.

MIXED BAG OF TRICKS

Do the least noticeable parts first. For example, the hood is one of the most noticed parts of a car. Do that last. Many times as the artwork process progresses, I find that my technique gets sharper as I get more used to it. It's not fun to have the highest degree of artwork on a portion of the car that won't be noticed as much. You want your work to be seen on the hood, the door panels, and the rear. Do those sections last.

Know your peak times of working ability and when you are at your sharpest. I used to put in 18-hour days and found that toward the end of that shift I made the most mistakes. Save nonpeak hours for maintenance, like cleaning airbrushes and bottles, filing duties, etc.

Take care when wiping down finished artwork with precleaner! Some painters use a mix of precleaner and water. Some companies make a product designed just for that purpose, like HOK's KC-20. I never use precleaner on any uncleared artwork. Since I use such thin paint mixtures, I seldom use base coat clear to seal my artwork. It tends to wash out, mottle, or dull the artwork. I'll carefully wipe precleaner around the artwork, removing any frisket adhesive.

When papering off completed portions of artwork to protect them from dripping airbrushes, I always cover the paper with masking tape. It forms a hard barrier that paint won't bleed through. I don't like to stick much tape to the artwork as problems can arise.

Try not to keep cars or parts in the work area of your shop other than what you're working on. If possible, have a separate storage area for them. If that is not possible, keep

HANDY HINT

Choosing stripe colors can be easy or difficult and can make all the difference in the success of a paint job. Sometimes I find that contrasting colors work best. But some base colors are more effective with stripes that are of a similar tone.

HANDY HINT

Things that should not be kept in a paint shop:

1. Silicone-based products like tire shine or antisqueak lubricants.
2. Open flames. Running kerosene heaters + a shop full of fumes = BOOM!
3. Open cans of paint products. Always seal those cans up and keep them in a paint cabinet.
4. Greasy foods. Actually, if you want to get serious, no food should be kept in the shop.
5. Hard liquor. At least wait until the work is done and the compressor is shut off.
6. Loaded guns. Never a good idea, they can lead to holes in cars, and nearby "car experts" and may be deadly when mixed with Number 5.

Also remember, if you are using a kerosene heater in your shop, residue from a poorly functioning heater (besides being dangerous) will be in the air and may land on the surface of the parts, causing contamination that may have an effect on the paint. Watch out what you spray in the shop. Never, never, spray any silicone- or oil-based product in the area you'll be painting in. It will cause fish eyes in the paint and also cause the painter to lose his or her mind. Another good reason not to keep loaded guns in the shop.

the cars or parts well covered. The chances of getting overspray on them are very good, even if you have an awesome ventilation system.

Also, overspray can get on the part that's being worked on. If I'm working on the left side of a car and have one side finished, I take a digital picture. Then paper off that side to protect it. I'll load the picture into my computer and reverse it with a graphics program. Even Microsoft Paint will work. Now it can be printed out and used as a reference for the right side of the car.

No camera? Keep the bottom of the paper loose, so you can go around the car, lift the paper, and peek under it.

When painting shadows under flames, graphics or anything, think of how the light hits the graphic to achieve that 3D effect.

Sometimes I find that it is easier to airbrush in a certain direction. For me, I airbrush better horizontally, back and forth, than I do vertically, up and down. Think about when you're about to airbrush a difficult surface and try to find an easier way. For example, in most cases I remove the hood and/or trunk lids off cars before airbrushing them. I seldom paint them while installed. I'll prop them on an artist's easel and do the airbrushing. If the artwork will wander from the part onto other surfaces of the car, I'll mount them back on the car and continue the artwork.

With gravity-feed airbrushes, it is easy to spill paint. If paint had dripped onto an already cleared surface, let it dry, then damp sand it off with 800-grit. Don't use solvent. If paint has dripped on freshly laid artwork, let it dry. Then airbrush over it. Rework that area. If it has dripped on a flame and run over onto the cleared base coat, respray that part of the flame and then damp sand the drip off the base coat. This is why I love having urethane clear over my base coats or finished

artwork. Lots of room for boo-boos. Many times the outline of the drip will still be visible, but after a round of clear coat and little more retouching, it will disappear.

I keep two mixtures of each color I am using at that time, a thicker one for darker shading, and a thinner mix for less grainy, lighter shading. Sometimes I even have three mixes, usually for black and white.

Always pull tape back against itself, breaking the paint edge. Don't wait too long to remove tape. The number of coats that were applied will determine how long before the tape can be pulled up. Not waiting long enough can result in the tape lifting the paint off the painted surface because the layers are too fresh. Wait too long and the paint will chip and splinter.

If the paint edge is very thick and a "bridge" has formed between the tape and paint surface, use EXTREME CARE. Cut along the tape line with a very sharp X-Acto Number 11 stencil knife. The tweezers will help to lift away the cut paint. Then pull up the tape. If the paint had dried too much, use a razor blade or stencil knife and carefully slice along the tape edge. Then use the tweezers to lift away the paint crust.

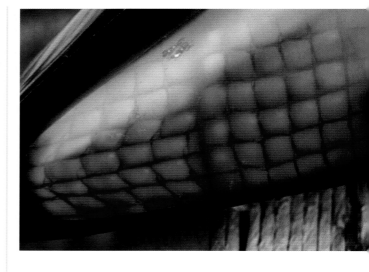

Don't limit what can be used as a tool. Here I used netting from an onion bag to airbrush gator skin.

If dealing with a very thick paint edge, use a razor blade to trim it down. Of course, this only works properly if a pinstripe will be applied. Sometimes a paint edge is so thick that the weight of clear coats can fold it over and air can get trapped underneath. I always trim thick paint edges down. I hold the razor at a shallow angle, not letting the razor touch anything other than the top of the paint edge, and slowly and carefully shave it down. If there is a raggy loose edge, I remove the excess material by either trimming it with a stencil knife or sticking masking tape against it, then pulling it up. The paint crust will come up with the tape.

To remove bits of adhesive residue from leaving masking tape on way too long, use precleaner.

Beware of using precleaner on uncleared artwork. The cleaner can penetrate and soften the paint, and you'll be removing artwork. I've actually seen marks from wiping with precleaner cause artwork residue to "wipe" across base coat.

If you're using base coat for airbrushing, the reduced paint will break down after a while. So if the airbrush spray is getting grainy, mix up a new batch. To aid in getting that photorealistic look, try to use photos of the subject being airbrushed. I even tape the photo right next to where I am airbrushing. Put the photo in a plastic bag to protect it.

Always do what I call a wet sand paint check after the artwork is done and stencils are removed. Very closely look over the car in the sun. With 800-grit, very, very carefully wet sand everything that doesn't have artwork on it. If the artwork doesn't have a sharp or distinct edge to it, don't even come close to the border of the fade. For example, if

the mural is of a sky that blends out from the base color, don't sand that blend. What you're doing is checking for any contamination that has happened during the artwork process. Overspray, paint that snuck past tape lines, pencil lines, whatever. Do this in the sun, because the sun will show every little booger. And for pencil or design lines, look very carefully along the edges of flames and graphics. Fold the sandpaper over so you have nice neat edge, and if you see a line, you can softly sand right up to the edge of that line without touching it.

There are times when the artwork must be designed around the spaces in which tools will fit on a car. For example, on the 1932 Ford seen in Chapter 6, area between the engine compartment panels and the front fenders is so limited in space that an airbrush doesn't even fit in there and the parts cannot be removed without major hassles. So artwork must be designed to accommodate that area. Or, as in that case, the engine panels (the side of the car) could be removed, rather than the fenders. Before designing the artwork for a car, look the car over, and know where the areas are that could crop up as problems to work on. Here I was able to remove the panels, but there are times when that is not an option.

CHAPTER 6
LOW-TECH WAYS TO DESIGN YOUR PAINT

I did not custom paint my first cars. Well, it was nothing that would be thought of as custom. I wanted those paint jobs to bring out the best features of the cars. I often look over a car and try to imagine the most effective way to bring out the lines of the car. A car with an awkward shape can be manipulated with artwork. The right design can, in a sense, reshape the car. And that was my primary goal when I began painting cars.

This is where having a reference library can come in handy. Keeping files of reference photos on your computer can be a real time saver. Most of these step-by-step chapters

include the drawings and explain how I made them, following the path the design took as it was being developed.

These days there are a few ways to work out the design prior to actually painting it on the car. It can be drawn out by hand or worked out on computer. There are even computer programs that allow you to load in the image of a car, and the program will work out the different designs and try out various colors on those designs. Most custom painters use what works best for them. I tend to draw things out by hand using the color copy blank method I describe in the previous chapter.

This artwork took a journey before it ever was painted on this 1932 Ford.

HANDY HINT

When designing any paint scheme, don't overlook areas such as the inside of the engine compartment. As people look over the vehicle, the "Oomph" factor goes up when they discover more cool artwork as doors, hoods, and trunklids are opened. Here the underside of a hood on a 1932 Ford is flamed.

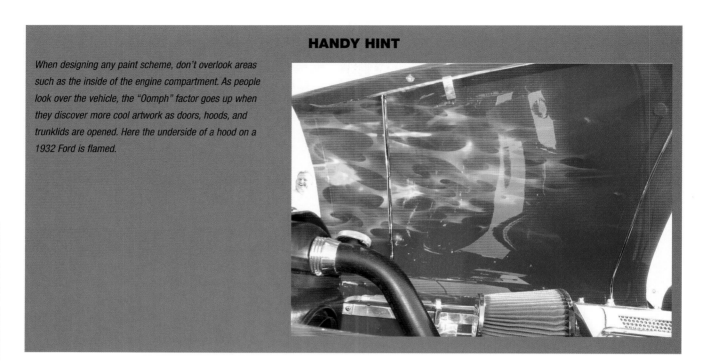

DRAWING DESIGNS BY HAND

I'll take a photo of a car, trace it, then use a copier to enlarge the traced drawing and make copies of it. Then I can play around, draw on the copies, and come up with the best artwork for the project. The owner of this "light red" hot rod loved the color. It was the color he wanted, but unfortunately the car wasn't getting any attention at shows.

Here I made an enlarged paper copy and then drew the flame shape on it. Next I cut that out and created a white area. The copy is placed on a scanner and a bunch of blanks are made.

Next, I play with colors using a simple computer graphics program. Sometimes the best color to use is one with a tone that is similar to the base coat. Not the case here—the purple doesn't fly.

This lime yellow/green is pretty wild. This is what I would use. But it's not my car. And the customer doesn't like it.

I filled the flames with yellow on the computer, printed it out, and used colored pencils for the orange fade around the flames and the blue pinstripe. He decides to go with the traditional flame colors of orange and yellow. With the drawings of sample color choices, he won't wonder what it could have looked like in a different color. I spent a morning playing around with these, and it was time well spent. The drawings look rough, but they do their job. And it was done fast.

The finished hot rod. He won the first show he entered after the flames were done. The flames really woke up the car and drew attention to all the fab work done to the front end.

Stan Springs was always saying he wanted me to paint flames on one of his hot rods, and then he'd change his mind. So this time I took a photo and made a few drawings, using the same technique I used with the pink car.

Here is the "blank" drawing I made. I really liked the way flames look on this car.

SKETCHING BY COMPUTER

Be warned, I am not an expert at computer graphics. I'm not even an amateur. So the following pictures are quite rough. Someday I may be better, but that day is not here yet. They are meant to inspire you and remind you that not everyone pops out of the box knowing how to do everything well. Eventually my Photoshop skills will improve. This chapter is not meant to be a lesson in Photoshop, so I am not specific in exactly how I made these drawings.

If you want to learn Photoshop, my advice is to take a course. Or find a graphic designer/artist friend, buy her or him dinner, and have them give you a few Photoshop lessons.

The design featured in this step-by-step involves a type of realistic flame painting. Chapter 7 is a full-blown step-by-step lesson of that technique, while this chapter focuses on the design process.

Here I did the flames in the traditional hot rod colors of yellow and orange using colored pencils. But Stan saw the drawing and decided the flames would be too overpowering, so the car was left in plain red. I mean, it was a cool car. It's not about whether it should have had flames on it. Some people might look at a design and say "That's too much." And others would say, "That is too cool." It's all a matter of personal preference. I liked the green flames on the pink car and the orange/yellow flames on Stan's car. But the customer wanted something else. In the end, I'm glad we went with the yellow flames on the pink street rod.

Here is what I started with. This car was painted a vivid red but needed something more, as there are red street rods everywhere. The customer, Raymond, wanted realistic flames. I had painted them on his 1939 street rod (refer to Chapter 7) and he wanted a less aggressive version of them on this car, just enough to break up the red and sleek out the lines of the car. He also wanted the design only on certain areas of the car, and the areas without artwork would not be receiving any sanding or clear. So this was taken into consideration during the design process.

Here is a photo of some flames from the 1939. I'll start Photoshop and open up a photo of the red car and one of these flames. Then I'll use Photoshop and "cut out" these flames with the Polygonal Lasso tool and hit "Copy."

Left: *I'll click on the red car, change over to that picture, then left click and hit "Paste." The copied flames from the black car will show up on the red car picture. Then I go to the top of the Photoshop window and hit "Edit." The drop-down menu will come up, and I'll click on "Free Transform."*

A box will come up around the pasted image. There are little boxes along the sides of the box. By moving the curser around these boxes, arrows will pop up. By clicking on and moving these arrows around, you can turn the box or make it longer or shorter. In short, you can manipulate the pasted image and make it fit what you want. I took these flames and made the pasted image longer. Then I pasted on more flames and used the "Free Transform" function on them and placed them where I wanted. I also could have used the Blur tool to soften the edges and blend the layers of flames. **Below left:** *Here's another version of the car with more flames pasted on.*

Right: *Another version of the flames. This time I'll angle them. First I paste on the cut-out flames.*
Below right: *I use the "Free Transform" function to resize and position the flames, and add more flames. Now I have several versions for the customer to choose from. He goes with the minimal flames that go straight across the car. No angle.*

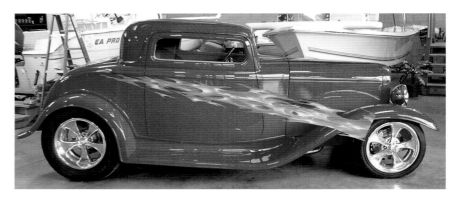

Above left: *Only the panels of the car that will receive artwork are prepped for artwork. The car is wiped down with a strong precleaner like HOK's KC-10. Wet down one cloth and wipe, then immediately wipe that up with a dry cloth. Repeat until the surface squeaks. Next, the panels are wet sanded with 800-grit paper.*
Above right: *3M Soft Edge Foam Masking Tape is run along the doorjamb, sticky side down, of course. It is a foam tape that has adhesive along one side. It sticks to and fills narrow areas like doorjambs, and trunk and hood edges. It will keep artwork overspray from getting into the doorjambs. I stick it along the edge and shut the door.*

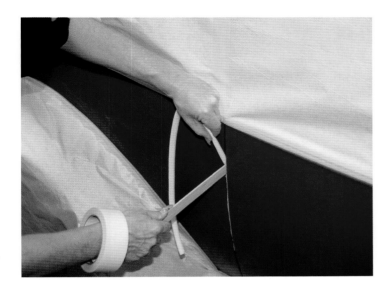

Not all of the doorjamb is reachable when the door is open. Using a paint paddle, I force the Soft Edge tape between the door and fender. This takes a little patience to get the sticky side down and have the foam not sticking into the crack. I pull up on it, stretch it, then push it down with the paddle.

Note how some panels, like the roof, fenders, and trunk area, are carefully masked off. These areas won't be getting any additional paint on them, and that includes no clear. So these surfaces won't be getting any sanding. That means no paint, no drips, and no overspray of any kind can get on these surfaces. One problem is the paint edge that will form once the clear is applied on the panels that get artwork. But we are lucky here, as there is a trim line that runs along the car. The "no artwork" surfaces are taped off along the corner of the crease of the trim line, so the paint edge will be camouflaged in the crease.

Now, some may wonder why the front fenders were not removed from this car. They are really in the way, and they make it hard to work on the sides of the engine compartment. But it became clear that removing them would involve disassembling almost the entire front end. So the fenders were left in place, and I managed to work around them.

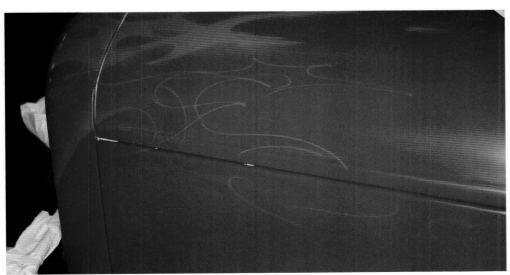

This realistic flame paint is very different from the flame paint seen in Chapter 7. It was very minimal and has almost an abstract graphic effect to it. I loosely sketched the flames using House of Kolor SG103 Molly Orange. For a full list of equipment and materials, see Chapter 7.

I keep reference photos close by when I'm working. This makes it easier to get the flames to look the way I want them to. My customer keeps telling me "less is more." So I am very careful not to overdo it. It's very easy to get carried away and end up with too much artwork. So I spend a lot of time stepping back and looking at what I've done so far.

The flame design is tapered off as it goes back across the car. There won't be very much more flame than is seen here. Next, I'll carefully layer candy colors over the orange flames and then bring in a few yellow flames, building them off of the orange flames.

Because the front end was left on the car, it is difficult to work on the lower areas of the grille shroud. The design will come all the way to the bottom of the shroud and the sides of the engine compartment. I look at the areas and patiently figure out how to angle the airbrush to reach these surfaces.

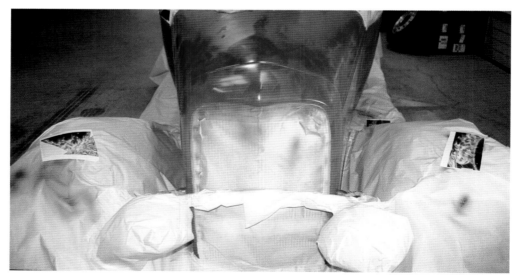

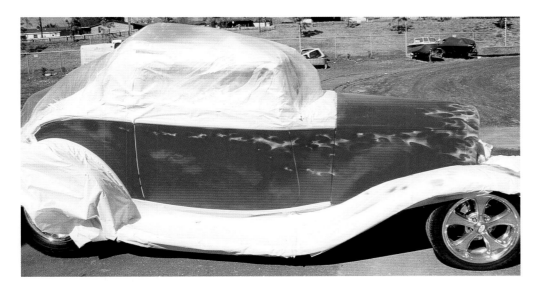

Now, since I had not tried this technique on red before, I wanted to see how it looked in the sun. I was looking to see if there was a dark shadow around the design. The design is mostly sprayed freehand, and some overspray will surround the artwork. The car is carefully rolled outside and it looks great. No distinct shadow, but the slight overlap of the candy on the red base adds a slight shadow that seems to "lift" the flame above the surface and give it a 3D effect. Unexpected and very cool!

See how there is very little airbrushing done behind those fenders? I'm lucky, as these side panels are easily removed. As the layout and angle of the design is complete, it's pretty simple to continue the design on the lower portion of the panels once they are removed. A big part of applying artwork on cars and trucks, especially older models, is figuring out how to work on the car. What areas will be painted on? Is anything obstructing the work surface? Can the obstruction be removed? Can the panel be removed to work on? Now these side panels are set on a table and easily airbrushed.

The car is cleared in pieces. The body is cleared separately from the hood and side panels.

Here are a few shots of the finished car. The car has gone on to win numerous awards, including Best Flames at the Good Guys Nationals.

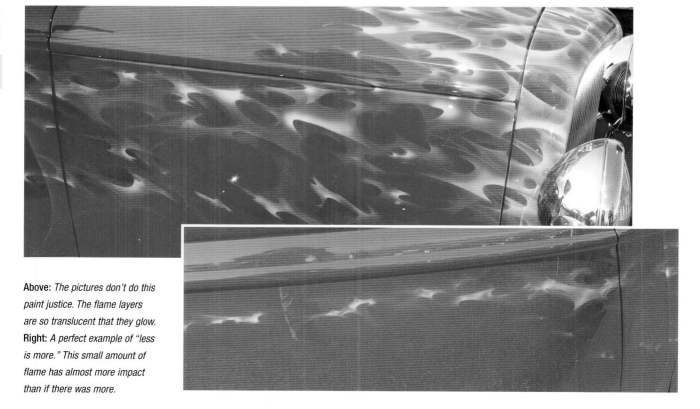

Above: *The pictures don't do this paint justice. The flame layers are so translucent that they glow.* **Right:** *A perfect example of "less is more." This small amount of flame has almost more impact than if there was more.*

CHAPTER 7
PAINTING REALISTIC FLAMES AND FUN WITH FIBERGLASS BODIES

Real flame painting has been around for years, but it has only been recently that it has become nearly as popular as traditional-style flames. Realistic flames can be painted on almost any color, but it tends to be more effective when painted over dark colors. A black base coat provides the most dramatic effect.

My "canvas" for these flames was a 1939 Ford street rod. It was a challenge, as I had never done this style of flame before. A month prior to painting this car I had the honor of visiting the shop of Mike Lavalle, the artist who pioneered the techniques for realistic flame painting. I was lucky enough to visit the shop on a day he was painting real flames. It was intense and inspiring watching him bring fire to life on the hood of a Corvette.

The techniques are simple, yet it takes a while getting used to them in order to get the most effective result. Now, I can't paint real flames like he does. My real fire technique is more of a "razor" flame. Every painter will develop the style that suits him or her best. Remember, the more you paint them, the better your technique will get, and the more your flames will look like real fire. Try to find reference photos of actual flames or take photos of a fire yourself. Look at the way the flames dance across the photo, how they are shaped. If you're trying this for the first time, practice your real flame technique on an old panel. Don't just jump onto a car like I did here. My nerves could hardly take it, as I had no idea if I could pull this off. And there were times when I thought I was in way over my head with this project.

MATERIAL AND EQUIPMENT

Artool Freehand Shields
SATA 2000 Digital Spray Gun
SATAgraph 3 airbrush
SATAminijet 4 spray gun
Iwata HPC airbrush
Rubber blocks
3M Soft Edge Foam masking tape
3/4- and 2-inch green masking tape
Masking paper and masking plastic
House of Kolor SG 103 Molly Orange
House of Kolor SG 102 ChromeYellow
House of Kolor KK-11 Apple Red Kandy Koncentrate
House of Kolor KK-08 Tangerine Kandy Koncentrate
House of Kolor KK-12 Pagan Gold Kandy Koncentrate.
House of Kolor SG-100 Intercoat Clear
800- and 600-grit sandpaper
House of Kolor KC 20 Post Paint precleaner
Gerson Blend Prep Tack Cloths
EZ-Mix Cups
Coast Airbrush's solvent-proof mixing bottles

The fiberglass body would be a challenge unto itself. Fiberglass has the tendency to have a great deal of static electricity. This means that dust, paint overspray, and nearly anything in the air will want to stick to the surface. I practically had to paint the flames with the airbrush in one hand and tack rag in the other. Painters have tried to find ways to deal with this problem for years. They've tried everything from grounding the car body (how do you ground fiberglass?) to washing water over the inner surface (doesn't work if the interior is assembled in the car).

Plus there was the little matter of the customer, Raymond Mays, putting mucho dinero into this car to tour with it at car shows across the country. Raymond is notorious for being extremely hard to please. And there was the fact that it seemed like everyone in North Carolina who had ever seen a car had heard about me painting realistic flames on this beast and wanted to stop by the shop to watch me work while they discussed exactly what they thought about the whole thing. So in addition to attempting to do a paint style I had no experience with on a car body that attracted every piece of debris within a mile, and a customer who was brutally critical, I was now doing it in front of an audience. No, no pressure at all! So have fun with me as I take you on what was, at the time, a journey through painting hell.

This is what the body of the car looked like before it was painted black. This is what I would use to draw up my ideas. I scanned the photo into my computer and used it to work up idea drawings to show Raymond.

Before I paint artwork on any vehicle, I first work out my ideas on paper or, in this case, Photoshop. This project was my first endeavor with Photoshop. My first try at working up a drawing was not bad for a first attempt. But I wanted a more polished image to show my customer. This can also be done by hand with drawings if you don't have a computer or Photoshop. I didn't know much. I basically blundered my way through this very rough drawing. Using the program, the car was "painted" black. I cut fire from other pictures on my computer. Then I cut, pasted, and manipulated ("Free Transform" in Photoshop language) the fire on the drawing of the car.

I went out and bought a book about Photoshop, then I tried again and came up with this drawing. Hmm . . . maybe I should have taken a class. I used my new drawing to make three versions, each showing different amounts of flame on the hood of the car, as that was the area that the customer was not sure about. Raymond was pleased and wanted a medium amount of flames on the hood. He was not 100 percent sure of this whole idea, but the more he saw, the more comfortable he became. He started to get excited about his paint.

The body of the car has been wet sanded with 600 and taped off. It has been mounted on a jig with wheels. This project will be less of a hassle, as the body is not installed on the frame. This makes it easy to move around and easy to mask off. There's no interior or motor to get overspray on. The only surface without paper or masking tape is the area being painted. Notice how the engine compartment is masked off. I previously did flames on the firewall. The nose was completely removed for that step. Then it was reassembled onto the car along with the front fenders.

The door jams have been masked off with 3M Soft Edge Foam Masking Tape. It is a foam that has adhesive along one side. It sticks to and fills narrow areas like door jams, and trunk and hood edges. This is a real timesaver. It will keep artwork overspray from getting into the door jams. I simply stick it along the edge and shut the door.

The area where the sides of the car's "nose" curves up and creates an area under the hood. This area will receive artwork. I don't want the hood to close all the way while I'm painting. Plus, I'll need to have access to the corners of the engine compartment. That is, where the sides of the car curve up under the hood. I'll want the flames to wrap around the corner into these areas. So I tape rubber blocks along those edges to hold the hood up. That way the paint doesn't get disturbed, and the hood doesn't latch. When the hood is up and I'm working on those areas, I'll remove the blocks and do my paintwork. I try to keep the blocks in areas that don't get much paint. Once I'm done with each flame layer in those areas, I'll let the paint dry then tape the blocks back in place. (Please note that this photo was taken out of sequence.)

Here are the Artool freehand stencils I will use along with some of the House of Kolor paint. The Matchmaker set has four stencils that fit together. So you can use them to get both sides of a curve. There is a positive and negative side of each curve. I also use the Essential Seven shield set as well as the S.P. Radu Vera Master Series, which includes the Bird and Pharaoh. More about exactly how these are used a little later. Since this car was painted, Artool has released a series of freehand shields specifically made for real fire flames designed by Mike Lavelle.

The hardest part is laying out the design on the car itself. I taped enlarged copies of the drawings close by for reference, but the design changed and morphed as I airbrushed the flame layout on the car. I started with Blue Blood red base coat thinned down to about 1 part base coat to 1 ½ to 2 parts reducer. I actually draw out the flame with the airbrush. Normally I run about 15 to 30 pounds of air pressure at my airbrush. But I find to get the best effect for this style of flame on a large surface like a car, I'll run 65 pounds.

Hold up a freehand shield and line it up with curves on the layout drawings on the car. Then spray against various curves on the stencil. Don't hold the airbrush right against the stencil. Keep it back. You want the image distinct in some places but not everywhere, and not too defined. I'll move the stencil around and spray. I'll take it away and dust on more paint, keeping the design somewhat diffused and loose.

Right: *Starting to fill in the lines.* **Below:** *See what I mean by diffused and not distinct? There would be several layers of flames, and the bottom layers had to be surreal and indistinct. This was a good base for my flames. I wiped the surface down with a tack rag every few minutes, as the overspray was a problem. Plus, after finishing each layer, I wiped over the surface with a gentle postsanding precleaner such as House of Kolor, KC-20. Don't saturate the surface.*

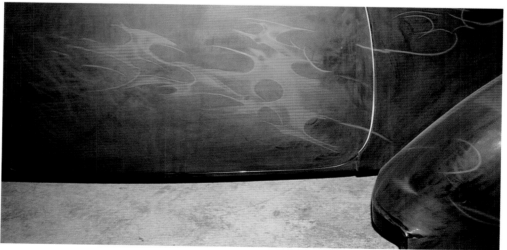

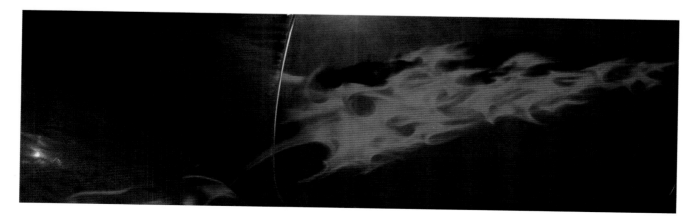

I worked my way toward the front of the car. Dang, those front fenders are huge! Lots of surface area there. Don't forget to tack rag! Notice how I used a body shop panel stand as my work area. I placed a board over it, covered it with masking paper, and taped airbrush holders to it. I can hang up my airbrushes, the paint bottles sit up top, and I can move this bench around behind me as I work my way around the car.

Notice how I lifted up the hood and continued the flames into the cowl. Once the orange layer of flames was complete, I tack ragged the exposed area and mixed up Apple Red candy concentrate into some intercoat or basecoat clear. As for how much concentrate to mix in, it's a matter of personal preference. I went for a medium mix, not too dark, not too light. I strained that mix into my SATAminijet 4 and, using a medium wide pattern, I applied a few layers of the red candy mix. Not too heavy, as I didn't want to disturb the red base coat flames, but enough to evenly apply color over the flames. Don't worry about getting red candy on the black. A glow of sorts is desired around the flames. But don't go too far past the flame area with the red candy.

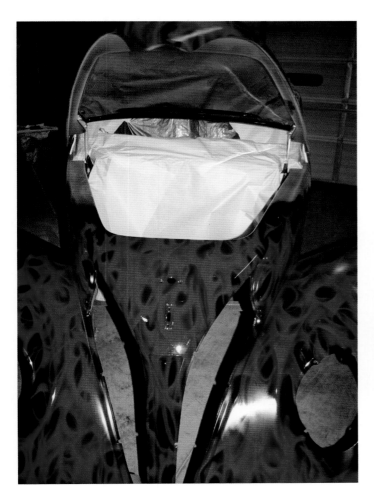

Me and my tack rag! Don't forget to tack rag in between coats of red candy. You'll know when it's time. You'll see the overspray sticking everywhere.

81

Next, I started airbrushing another layer of flames with Molly Orange basecoat. I drew out the flame shapes with the airbrush.

Then, with the freehand shields, I started filling in the flames. I still kept my design fairly loose. I tend not to go back and forth along the edge of the stencil. Rather, I move the airbrush in random motions around, directing the spray toward the area of the stencil I am using.

Here's a front fender with the orange base coat flame layer complete. I'm not sure I like it.

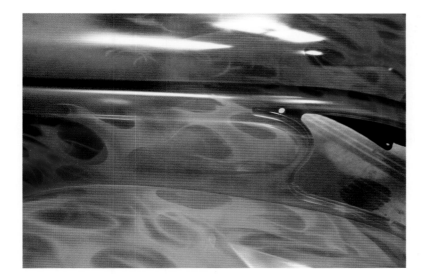

Here's the side of the engine compartment where it meets up with the fender. In order to reach that area, which is a 90-degree angle, I placed the freehand shields right up against the opposing part and sprayed with the airbrush. I like the way the movement of the flames is visible here. It truly flows. Note how I tried to make the artwork match up on both the side and the fender.

The completed second layer of flames. Notice how I allow some pieces of fire to break off? These little bits of fire really add the realistic fire effect. I'll continue to the very back of the car with these little bits of fire, making them smaller and smaller until they recede completely. I find I'm using fewer flames than on the red layer. The effect of moving flames is starting to show and there are certain areas of the flames that I like better than the others. The door flames are looking very good. I notice there's more black showing, and I think with less flame it appears more aggressive.

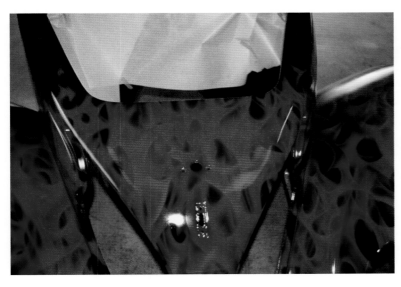

Now I'll layer on base coat clear with some candy tangerine orange concentrate mixed in using the minijet 4 spray gun. Note how there are fewer orange flames than red ones. It is very apparent on the engine cowl area, seen here. Don't forget to tack rag before spraying the orange candy.

The second layer of flames with the orange candy. They began to look much darker, and I wasn't sure I liked it. But I kept working.

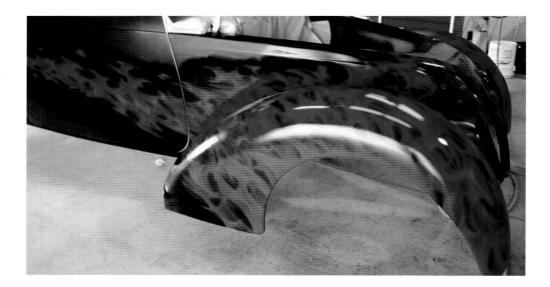

Starting the third layer. This time I used yellow base coat. I kept the mixture thin; I didn't want it to be grainy, as this would be the top and most visible layer. I also tried to keep the yellow layer as minimal as possible. On some areas I applied yellow flames right over parts of the orange flame, sometimes going over the same lines but then building a new flame off of that. The yellow layer should accent the other layers. And don't forget to tack rag!

See how the yellow flame is more an accent to the other layers? After a while you'll get the hang of building new flames off of existing ones. And if you do a flame part you don't like, the base coat is black. That means you can just "erase" the unwanted flame by airbrushing some black over it.

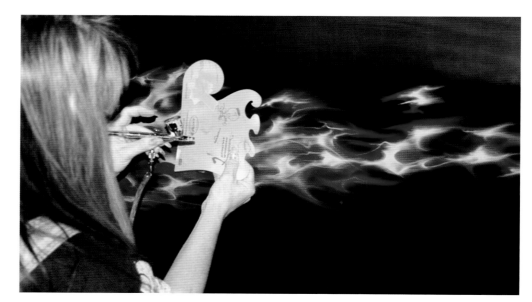

84

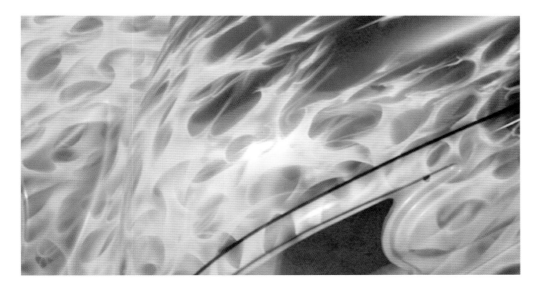

The yellow flames were working very well on the front section of the hood. I had the perfect mix of form and movement. I used a lot of freehand airbrushing and accenting with the freehand shields.

Above left: The yellow flame layer worked effectively down the side of the car and onto the door. It looked like I need to add a little more yellow flame down toward the bottom of the door. Above right: But I did not like the way the fenders were looking. They didn't have the flickery flame effect. It just looked too "loopy." Maybe I should have gone with less flame and more black base showing through. But to add more black, I'd need to do a lot of rework, and the clock was ticking. I decided to make it work . . . somehow. It's not that bad, but not nearly as effective as the hood or doors.

Next I accent the yellow layer with the candy orange mix. I'll just apply it over various areas of the yellow layer. I used the orange candy to deepen the layers to add depth when one flame goes under another and on some flame edges to give the flame depth. The fender on the left has been accented with the candy. Notice the difference it makes.

Here you can really see what I mean by using the orange candy to give the flames depth. is the orange candy is all freehanded in. I didn't use the shields here.

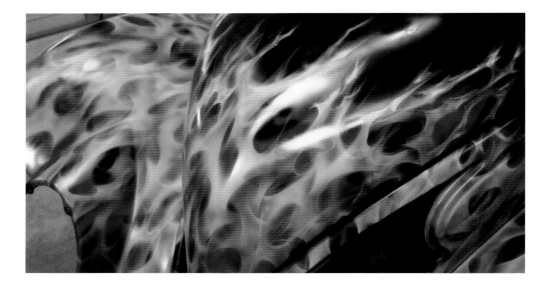

The fenders seemed to go from bad to worse. The hood and doors are so much better.

I tried accenting the edge of the fender with more yellow to get more of a fire effect, as if the hot fire was burning out from under the fenders.

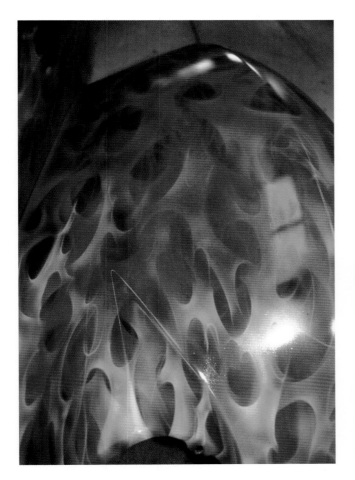

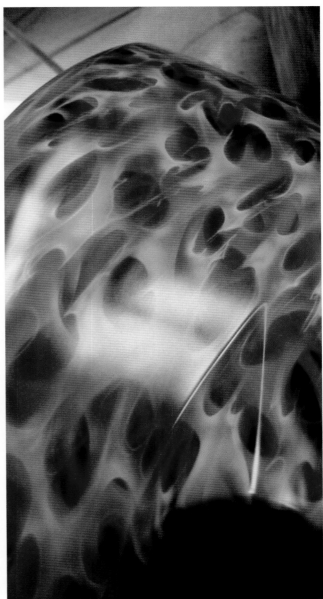

Left: *I decided to add another yellow layer on the fenders only. But first, I had to deepen and diffuse the yellow layer that is already there. I used the minijet and turned my pattern, air pressure, and fluid control way down, making the gun into a big airbrush of sorts. I softly spray on an orange layer but make it more random than even, darker in some places, lighter in others. This will help to separate the flames and help them to look more real.*

Below left: *This time I used a more aggressive, thinner flame, more like the ones on the doors and hood, sketching them in using the yellow. I gave them a flow that races across the fender surface. Raymond had shown up and was very pleased.*

Below: *Next, I accented the flames with orange candy. I already like it.*

I finished with the new yellow layer on one fender and started to apply the candy orange on the other fender to deepen and cover the old yellow layer. Don't forget to tack rag!

Next, I mixed House of Kolor Pagan Gold Kandy Koncentrate with their SG-100 Intercoat Clear. Using my SATAminijet, I sprayed a layer of this mix over everything. This color brought the flames to life, adding depth and richening all the colors. Don't mix it too dark. You can always add another coat of candy gold. And don't forget to tack rag before spraying this layer, as this will lock down any overspray and it will be very visible. It looks like the extra layer on the fenders worked. At this point I decided to stop and take a break. One of the problems with any artwork project is knowing when to stop painting. It is tempting to keep airbrushing and just add a little here and there. Yet, unfortunately, I'm not done yet.

Here's a close-up of the door flames. Notice how with each layer there are fewer flames and they become more distinct and sharp edged.

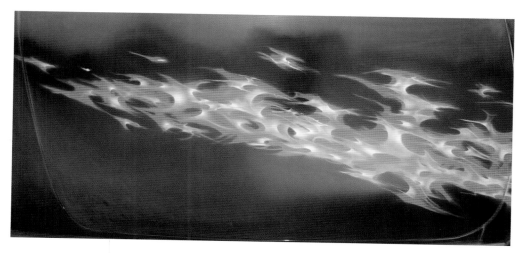

Not done yet! Now the running boards are "propped" in place. We put in a few bolts and rest the running boards on cardboard boxes, as the rear fenders of the car are not in place to bolt the boards to. Flames and bits of fire are airbrushed on the running boards. The fire from the fenders now runs across the running boards.

The fenders had to be removed. Notice how there isn't much yellow flame on the sides? I knew I'd be doing this step, and I didn't want too much yellow flame. As this was a body only, it was easy to remove them. Assembled cars—those with engines, running gear, and lights all wired up—are a different story. It may not be so easy to remove the fenders for this step. If the fenders cannot be removed, extra care will have to be taken when airbrushing artwork on the area where the fenders meet up with the side of the car. In some cases, as with the 1932 Ford seen in Chapter 6, that area is so limited in space that an airbrush doesn't even fit in there. So artwork must be designed to accommodate that area. Or, as in that case, the engine panels (the sides of the car) could be removed rather than the fenders. Before designing the artwork for a car, look the car over and know where the areas are that could crop up as problems to work on.

With the fenders removed, I could airbrush the yellow flame. I took all the flame edges past the "line" where the fenders meet the sides of the car. This way, it looks all sharp and professional. See how far I'm holding the airbrush from the surface? This is why the paint has to be mixed on the thin side. If it were thick, the flames would have a grainy texture and there'd be a lot of overspray.

Above: *I also painted fire on the trunk lid. I painted the lid off the car, standing it up on an easel. Then it was carefully bolted in place and spaced out correctly. I continued the flames on the top and bottom of the area around the trunk lid. I did not like this first version I did.* **Right:** *I wet sanded those flames off and started from scratch. This picture was taken at the very end of the paint job after the clearcoat. This version of flames on the trunk lid is much better.*

The car so far! The flames are now done!

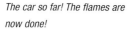

Even though I tack ragged the surface constantly as well as wiping it down with postpaint precleaner, I want to be sure there is no leftover paint from the flames beyond the artwork. There may also be spots of paint or debris that have landed onto the black base coat. So I wet sanded around the flame area with 800-grit paper. Take care not to come too close to the flame area. You don't want to ruin the soft glow that surrounds the flames. It is hard to see, but it is there.

Next, I loaded the base coat black in my airbrush and went around the flame edges and "trimmed" them. What I'm doing is helping the transition between the flame and the black. And there may be areas of the flame I don't like and want to adjust by blacking some of it out. Just be sure to watch for black overspray getting onto the flame area. You don't want that. Keep the tack rag handy and tack it often. Keep the pressure low for this step, about 35–40 pounds. I take every precaution to make sure I don't mess up all my flame work with black overspray. After you're done, wipe the whole car down with postpaint precleaner.

HANDY HINT

There is a glassy coat of black paint on the underside of parts like the hood, trunk lid, etc. This is the case with many custom painted cars. To keep overspray from the clear off these surfaces, the undersides are carefully masked off before the clear coat is sprayed.

91

With the body completely disassembled, the masking paper was removed and the car body was rolled into the paint booth for clear coat application. The fenders, nose, and hood were placed on stands in the booth and new masking paper was taped into place. The car body was cleared separately from the parts, as there is not enough room in the booth for everything.

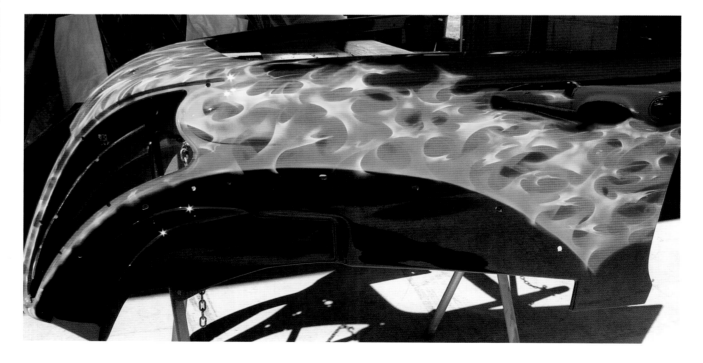

The nose of the car all cleared. Wow, the flames come to life! The various layers can all be seen, and it looks like it's on fire. You can see right through the yellow layer. This is one of the reasons I wanted the yellow mix to be thinner. Actual flames have a transparent look to them.

After carefully looking over the car parts in the bright sun, I found a few areas with some red overspray from the flames. I was so careful, but some did manage to sneak by. The fiberglass body attracts paint overspray like a magnet. The only way this was visible was with clear over it and could only be seen in the sunlight. I always try and have sunlight to check over my paintwork. Many flaws cannot be seen in the shop light. I took photos to keep track of the areas I had to retouch with black. Then I wet sanded with 800-grit and carefully applied a few black coats in those areas. After I finished, I carefully looked over the flames for black overspray and wet sanded it off.

Here's an overhead shot of the hood. The way the little bits of fire trail off of the main flames really brings the fire effect to life. I always find it very helpful to see intense close-ups of whatever technique I am learning. This photo really shows how transparent the layers are. How they build to create the illusion of real flames. The hood fire is my favorite part of the car. I feel this area came out the best.

Here's a gallery of various photos of the finished real fire flame paint. The car is not yet fully assembled.

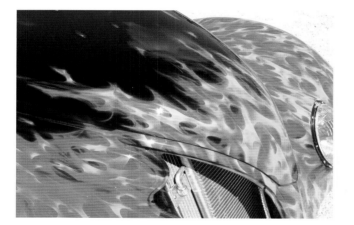

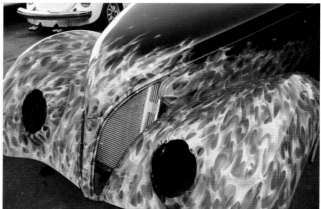

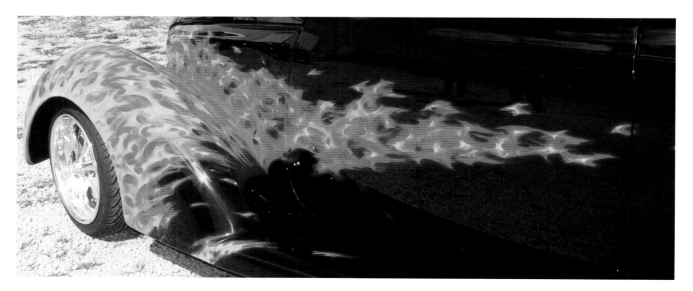

The gradual taper of the flames and the little bits of fire breaking off suits this design perfectly.

CHAPTER 8
METAL EFFECT TRIBAL GRAPHICS AND USING SPRAY MASK

One of the quickest and most effective graphic effects is what I call the metal effect technique. This is a painting technique that involves airbrushing black and white base coat to achieve an almost metal look to any kind of artwork, whether you're painting graphics, flames, or lettering. It's quick, it's easy, and it looks great. In this step-by-step, I'm airbrushing a tribal design on a Mini hood.

Tribal designs are fun to draw out, but it takes some getting used to. The artist needs to relax and let the design take shape. Before I was able to draw out tribal designs, I looked at hundreds of them. Tattoo magazines are a good source to becoming familiar with tribal designs. Also, sport truck magazines feature many trucks with tribal-style artwork. Look at the designs of others, and then draw up your own. Find your unique style of "tribal" and make it your signature.

There are many other ways to mask off a graphic. Transfer tape may also be used. Transfer tape comes in either opaque or clear and is mostly used in the sign industry for transferring vinyl graphics to a surface. But many artists use it as a masking material. The opaque version cuts easily and can be drawn on with a pencil. The clear transfer tape cuts a little harder, plus it doesn't stick as smoothly to the surface. But it has the advantage of being transparent. So if a painter is trying to apply a second layer of graphics or flames, and the placement of them is based on the previously applied layers, then clear transfer tape can be the way to go. Sheets of transfer tape are laid out over the panels receiving artwork.

Or, simply tape off a design with fineline tape and then mask with transfer tape or masking tape. Refer to Chapters 5, 9, and 10 for more information on those methods. How a design is masked off depends on the amount of area being worked on. For most large applications, such as the entire side of a car, fineline and masking tape and masking paper work best, here I'll be using spray mask.

Above left: *Here I've taken a hood with a marblized base coat and wet sanded it with 600 paper. I like using 600 for preparing a surface for artwork. It's fine enough so, in most cases, there are no sand scratches that show through, and it's rough enough that any paint layered over it sticks well, and further tape-outs won't result in lifting any artwork.* **Above right:** *Next I'll brush on a layer of MetalFlake Corporation Spray Mask, using a cheap 2-inch paint brush. I'll brush on four coats, allowing each coat to dry clear before applying the next.*

MATERIAL AND EQUIPMENT

MetalFlake Corporation Spray Mask
Transfer tape, Sticky Mickey brand available from
Eastwoodco.com
Auto mask from Coastairbrush.com
Tracing paper
Pencil
House of Kolor PBC43 Black Pearl
House of Kolor PBC49 Silverwhite Pearl
⅛-inch green fineline tape
¼-inch blue fineline tape
½-inch masking tape
White base coat

Black base coat
Stabilo pencils
Gerson Blend prep tack cloths
EZ-Mix cups
Coast Airbrush's solvent-proof mixing bottles
Measuring tape or steel ruler
X-Acto Number 4 knife
SATA 2000 Digital Spray Gun
SATAminijet 3 spray gun
SATAgraph 3 airbrush
Iwata HP-C airbrush
Uncle Bill's Sliver Gripper tweezers

Left: *Here I've taken a hood with a marblized base coat and covered it with tracing paper. The reason why? I like playing with my designs, fine-tuning them until they truly fit the space. This means I end up with lines all over the place, and it can get confusing trying to sort out the final design from all the undesired lines. This way I have room to maneuver and further rework the design without making a mess. If I were doing the whole side of a car and felt confident with the design, I'd just start measuring and then drawing out my design. But I'm fairly cautious, so chances are I'd cover the artwork areas with masking paper, and draw on that.*

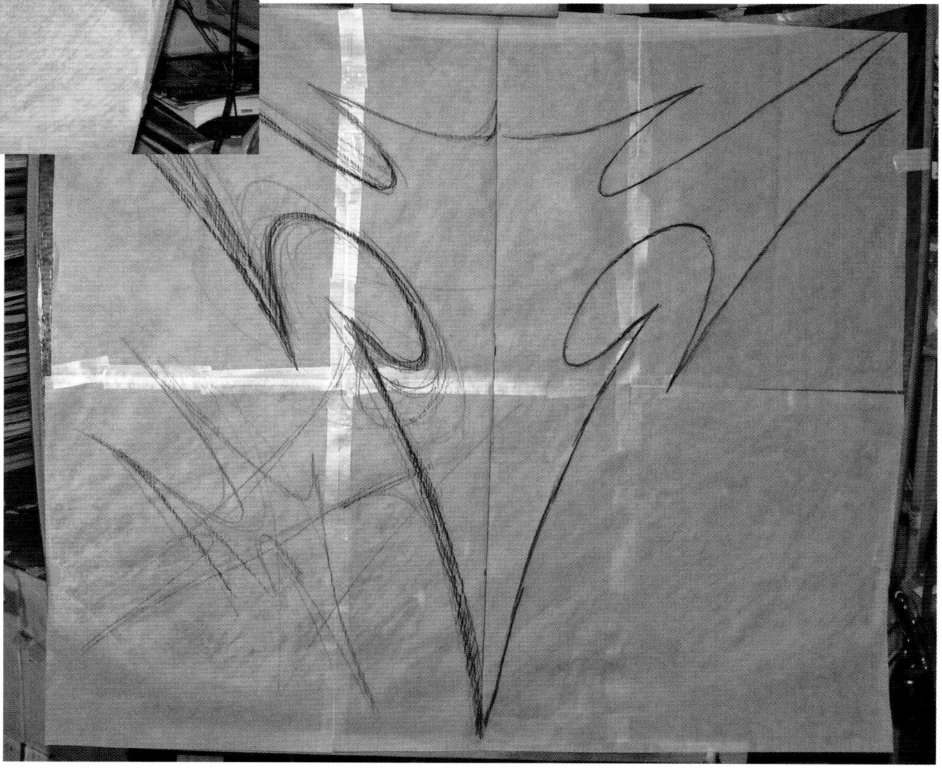

Right: *This is the end result design. I wanted something aggressive and edgy for this hood as it would be displayed at the SATA booth at the NACE trade show. I thought about having more designs on each side of the main design. You can see where I played around with that idea. The trick to getting both sides of the design to match is finding the centerline of the area being worked on. Draw the design on one side of that line. Then fold the paper over and trace away on the other side. The leftover lines from sketching out the design can be seen on the left side of the photo. The other side looks so clean because I just traced those lines from the left side.*

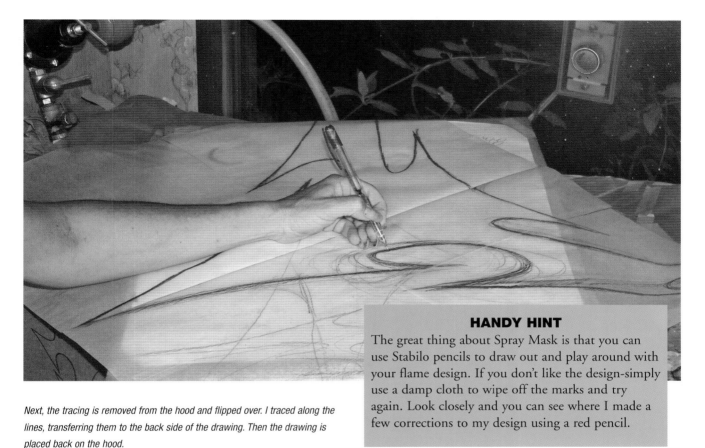

HANDY HINT

The great thing about Spray Mask is that you can use Stabilo pencils to draw out and play around with your flame design. If you don't like the design-simply use a damp cloth to wipe off the marks and try again. Look closely and you can see where I made a few corrections to my design using a red pencil.

Next, the tracing is removed from the hood and flipped over. I traced along the lines, transferring them to the back side of the drawing. Then the drawing is placed back on the hood.

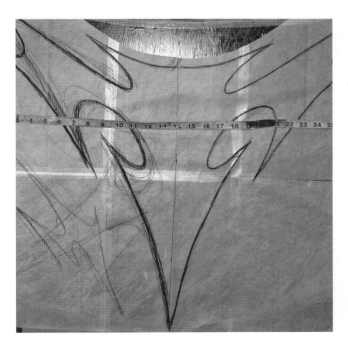

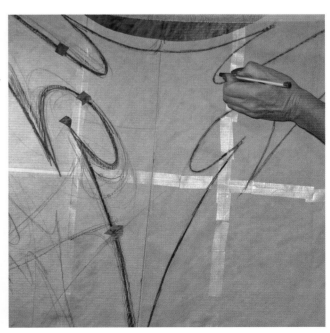

Above left: *I was never sure just how centered the drawing was on the hood. So now I take care to measure exactly where to place the centerline on the drawing. Using a measuring tape, I find the exact center of the hood and line up the centerlines.* **Above right:** *Then I trace along the lines with a pen, and the pencil-like material on the back transfers the lines to the surface of the hood.*

97

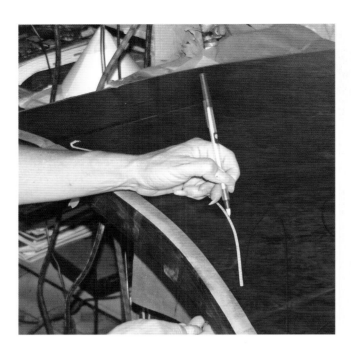

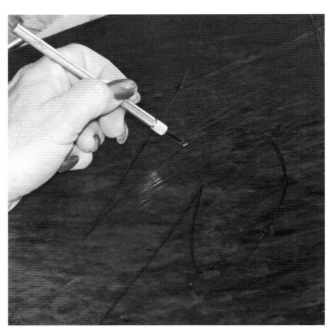

Above left: *Since I'm either a perfectionist or insane, I'll remove the drawing and go over all the pencil lines on the hood surface with ⅛-inch green fineline tape and a pen, redrawing the lines smoother and straighter.* **Above right:** *Using a Number 4 X-Acto knife, I carefully cut along the lines, attempting to cut through the Spray Mask but not into the surface of the hood. This is something that takes practice, knowing just how much pressure to apply when cutting. Whether cutting through Spray Mask or transfer tape, if you're new at cutting stencils like this, cut a little bit in an area that's hard to see, and check to see just how deeply the surface is being cut into. Lift the edge of stencil up and look at the cut.*

Now that the hood is all masked off, I use a SATAminijet 3 to spray two coats of black, then two coats of House of Kolor Pearls. I mix a little PBC43 Black Pearl into PBC49 Silverwhite Pearl. I'm trying to get a dark burnished platinum effect. A mini spray gun is perfect for spraying the background colors for graphics and flames.

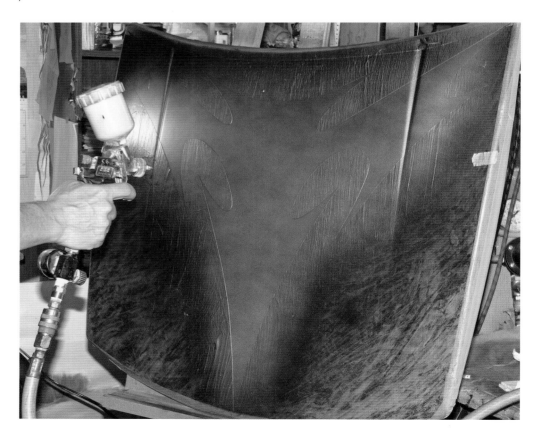

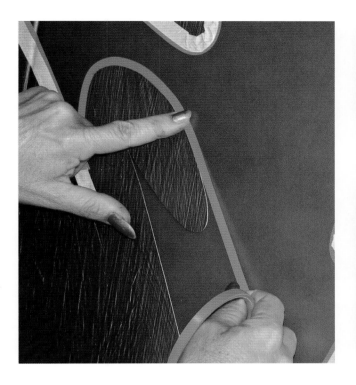

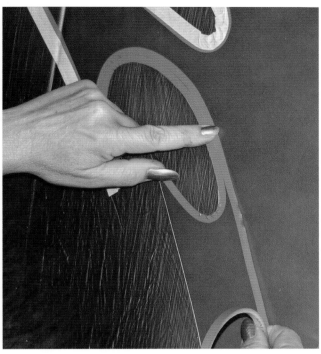

Above left: *Using ¼-inch blue fineline tape, I start to create a bevel around the edge of the design. The tape will allow me to get an even bevel width all the way around the design. It's a quick and easy way to measure out a border.* **Above right:** *To get a ½-inch bevel, I'll lay another strip of ¼-inch blue fineline alongside the first. Then I run ½-inch masking tape along and cover any gap between the two strips of blue tape.*

Above left: *With a steel ruler, I'll make some reference marks to help me keep the slant of the reflections even. I hold up the ruler, find the optimum angle of slant, and make two marks.* **Above right:** *Then I'll measure from the first marks and make two reference points.*

Then I can line up the two reference points using the steel ruler and draw a line. When I spray the reflections, I just have to follow along these lines and all the reflection angles will be the same across the design.

The trick to getting metal effect to look real is to find out how the light hits the design. I picture the light source coming from above and slightly to the right. That means the light will be hitting the lower edges of the design. Using an Iwata HP-C airbrush and white base coat thinned down 150 percent, I spray along those lower edges. Then I run the white across the design along the reference lines I drew earlier, keeping the white concentrated along the lower edges. I'll usually keep two mixtures of each color I use while airbrushing, one thicker mixture for overall color and another thinner one for shading. Thin the mixtures until the paint does not spray grainy.

Do the same thing in reverse using black base coat. Concentrate the black on the upper edges, and airbrush along the reflection lines next to the white ones. I'll usually go over the white again, fine-tuning it. Then I'll spray just enough black to cover any white overspray that has wandered into the darkest black areas.

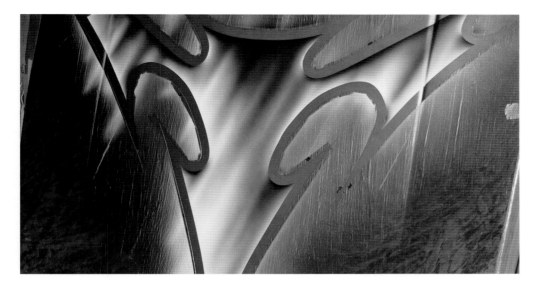

The border tape is pulled away and you can see the area that will become the bevel. The dimensional effect is already taking shape.

Now to shade the bevel. I tape off each individual area. First I'll use ⅛-inch green fineline tape to tape off the ends of the area, running it from corner to corner. I'm pointing to the "spike" in the design. I'll run the tape right down the center of that to the very point, cutting the spike in half.

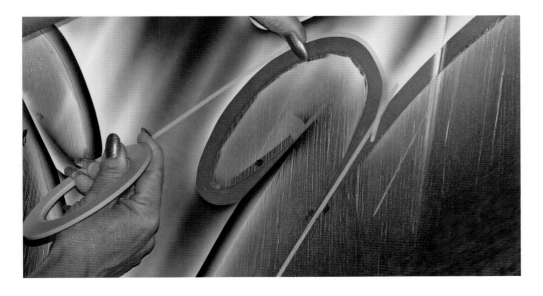

Now the fineline tape is run along the top edge. By looking at the areas of the bevel already shaded, you can see where this is going.

Above left: *The other side is taped off. In this close-up, you can clearly see how the tape slices right through the center.* **Above right:** *Now the rest of the area is masked off. Then white base coat is sprayed along the lower edge of the upper circle.*

Above left: *Then black base coat is sprayed along the upper edge of the bevel. As this is the bottom edge of the bevel, this side is in shadow.* **Above right:** *Next, the edge of the spike is sprayed with white. As it is the side of the spike that faces upward, it will reflect light.*

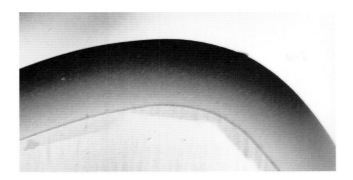

Above left: *The thing to watch out for will be little bits of paint that have snuck past any lifted edges of tape. This tends to happen on the sharp curves, where the tape will want to lift.* Above right: *After the graphic has dried, but not so dry that the edge flakes, I remove the stencil material. I'll use Uncle Bill's Sliver Gripper tweezers to gently lift the mask and pull it back. Always pull any mask material back against itself, breaking the paint edge. Remove the mask too soon and the paint might still be too pliable, and the edge won't want to cleanly break. Wait too long and the paint will be so hard it will chip away as the mask is being pulled up. This is where it is handy to be familiar with the material being used. That way you know about how long to wait. Also keep in mind that more coats of paint applied to flames or graphics means more time needed to dry, which means more time to wait before removing the mask. You'll notice an impression wherever the tape border around the Spray Mask was. I damp sand this away with 800, taking care not to touch the artwork.*

HANDY HINT
To remove Spray Mask that was applied too thinly to peel up, use a pink eraser or damp sand with 1,000-grit if it's on cleared basecoat.

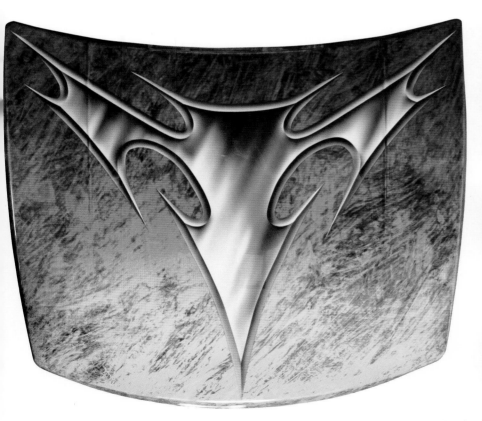

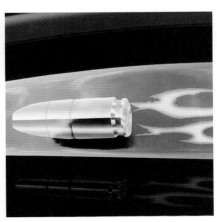

Above: *The finished hood. I had been thinking of putting a shadow under the blade design but decided against it, as it already had a "floaty" appearance. See how easy this effect is to airbrush? This technique could be used anywhere—in flames, graphics, and lettering, or mixed in with other techniques in multilayer graphics.* Top right: *Here's an example of metal effect used to airbrush tribal flames.* Above right: *The metal effect technique works great for this bullet mural.*

CHAPTER 9
GHOST FLAMES AND SILVER LEAF FLAMES

I'm not sure when the first flames were painted on cars, but it's a great way to bring out the wild, bold side of a vehicle, and it will never go out of style. There are so many ways to paint flames, and exciting new styles of flames and new flame techniques and designs are constantly being invented. There must be as many ways of painting flames as there are flame designs.

Flames can be masked in a variety of ways, including traditional tape-outs, liquid Spray Mask, transfer tape cutouts, and more. I'll try to cover a few popular techniques and styles in this chapter. Read through the processes here and the tips at the end. And don't be afraid to go beyond these "borders" and try something new. Who knows? You might come up with your own flame style.

GHOST FLAMES

The trick to doing ghost flames is simply spraying as light a line as possible around the edges of the taped-off flame. In custom painting, "ghost" means hard to see but visible. Traditionally, the perfect ghost flame is one that can only be seen from certain angles and in certain light. Usually it is the same tone as the base paint, only a lighter shade. For black base coat, you'd airbrush charcoal pearl for the ghost flame. For a candy blue base coat, a light blue pearl would be used.

The reason for using pearl instead of a solid color is that pearl dusts on with nice even coverage, while solid colors can break up and appear spotty. Plus, pearl has that shimmery effect that makes it very effective for ghost flames.

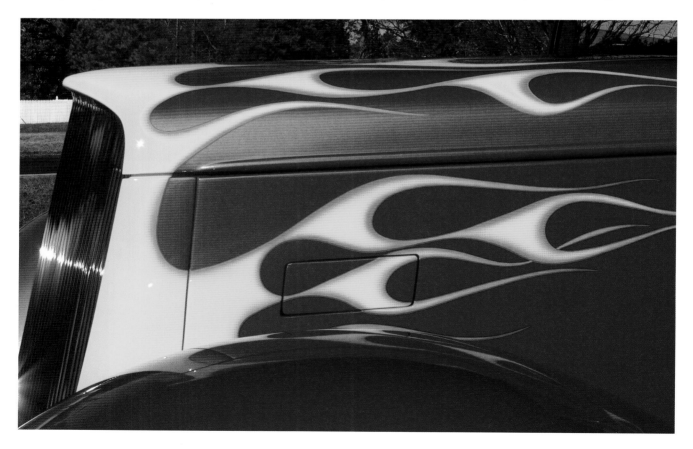

Traditional hot rod flames bring this street rod to life.

MATERIALS AND EQUIPMENT

Transfer tape
¾-inch masking tape
2-inch masking tape
½-inch masking tape
¼-inch masking tape
¹⁄₁₆-inch green fineline tape
Pencil eraser
600- or 800-grit sandpaper
Silver leaf
Mona Lisa Gold Leaf Adhesive
House of Kolor AP-01 Adhesion Promoter
Tracing paper
Pencil
Uncle Bill's Sliver Grippers (tweezers)SATA Jet 2000
Digital Spray gun
SATA Mini Jet 4 spray gun
SATA dekor artbrush
SATAgraph 3 airbrush
Iwata HP-C airbrush
Tape measure
Squirrel hair lettering brush
Scissors
Piece of velvet cloth

HANDY HINT

One thing to remember before starting any flame project is to stock up on plenty of tape, all kinds and in various widths. There is no such thing as too much tape. You will be surprised at how fast you'll go through it, especially on big cars or on trucks. And don't buy cheap tape. It will lift, and overspray will sneak under it and create more problems. When flaming large areas, it's very tempting to take shortcuts and save money on materials, but it's always a bad idea. Been there, and suffered the consequences.

This Miata is not the kind of car that is usually flamed. Old street rods and 1960s and 1970s muscle cars are the main canvases for flames. In fact, I had not even planned on doing flames on this car, but I was playing around and decided, "Why not?" The first step taken in this process was to take a digital photo of the car. The photo was loaded into my computer and several copies were made. Now, the low-tech way to do this would be take a photo of whatever vehicle you want to flame and make enlarged copies of it at any copy store.

Ghost flames are best done over pearl or metallic base coats or under candy or pearl colors. You can even mix a few ghost flames under a regular flame paint job. A neat trick is to do a reverse of the color order above, and use a dark color for the ghost flame on a lighter color base. For example, you might use a black ghost flame on a dark blue candy base coat.

Ghost effects also work great when painted in multiple layers. Using handheld shields and lightly spraying one layer of flames after another is a quick way to create a cool effect that will work for many kinds of artwork, whether it is used as a fade-in over a candy or pearl base coat or inside a graphic such as a taped-off tribal graphic, flame, or panel.

First, flames are drawn on the car in pencil. In this case I only did one drawing. The first version was perfect and I knew it when I drew it up. But I usually make up several versions. For most flame projects, the painter will want to see how different colors will look. So make several versions using various colors combinations.

When playing with colors for ghost flames, I simply draw on a copy with colored pencils, tracing over the flame outline. But for all those keyboard commandos out there, this step can easily be done on the computer. I'm too impatient. Most flame paint designs will not be ghosted, and you'll want to see solidly colored flames, not just outlines. Yet for this kind of drawing I still prefer to do most of it by hand. Use whatever method works for you. For "nonghost" flame drawings, I can either carefully paint out the flames on the copy with whiteout or I can cut them out. Then make copies of that. What I'm doing is making "flame blanks" that will be used to find the optimum flame colors. I'll either load the photo back into my computer and color it with a program like Photoshop or I'll just use color pencils to color in the flames. Refer to Chapter 6 for more information.

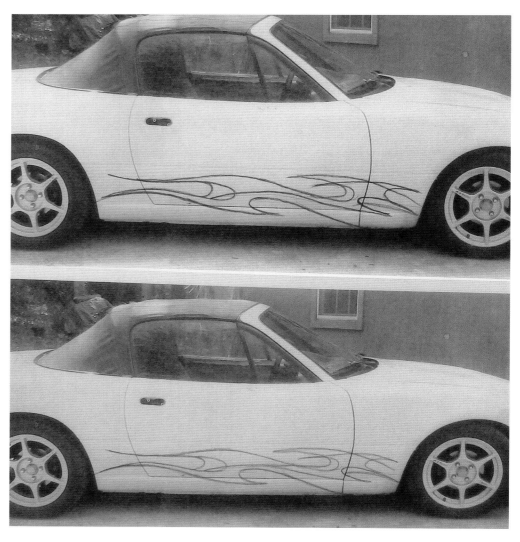

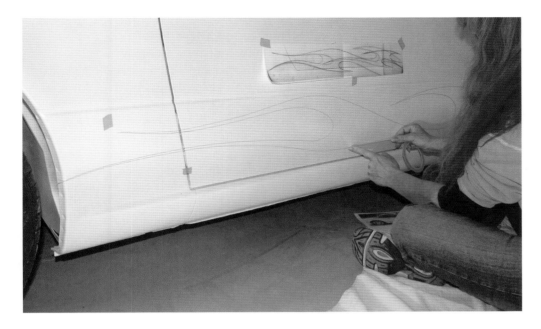

The traditional flame technique involves laying down a flame outline using a very thin tape. I tape off flames with 1/16-inch 3M green fineline tape. Some folks use 1/8-inch masking tape or blue fineline tape. Some use 1/16-inch green fineline tape. Everyone says their method is the best. I think folks just use what works best for them. Taping off the flame is the easy part. Note how I have a copy of the flame design taped above the design area, close by to refer to. I can use the door and fender lines on the drawing as a reference for laying out the flames.

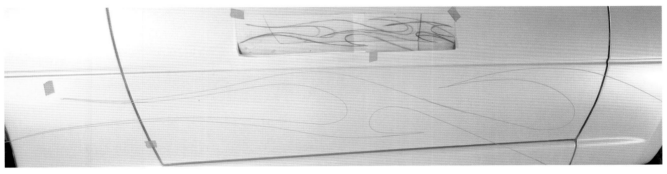

Arranging the flame design to best fit the contours of the panel is the hard part. Don't just rush through it. It is quite unpleasant to untape a car after hours of work and layers of paint to see that the design looks awkward or just doesn't complement the line of the sheet metal. I enjoy painting flames and like to have fun with designs. My main thing is to go for flame symmetry—having the flame design nicely balanced—not too generic, not too uniform, but not too busy.

I use two methods of laying out flames. With one, I layout the flame with 1/16-inch green fineline tape. I prefer it over the blue tape because it is stiffer and lays down a "smoother" flame line. Its advantage over the masking tape is that it leaves a crisp, sharp line, perfect for flames like ghost flames or metal effect flames which will not be pinstriped. Most folks who use masking tape pinstripe their flames. Once the flames are laid out, take a very short break. You don't want the taped corners to lift, but go get a cold drink and then go back and look at your design. Always stand back and study it. It's too easy to miss something obvious when only looking at it close up.

Normally I'd make a flame pattern. Refer to Chapter 10: Graphics for a detailed step-by-step on creating a pattern. But these are ghost flames, so using a pattern to transfer the design to the paint surface is not an option. The reason? They're ghost flames, and very, very transparent. Any pencil or chalk line will show, no matter how careful you are to remove it prior to painting. Some of the material will get stuck under the edge of the tape and get sealed down by the flame paint. But for regular flames, the pattern technique works great, especially for reversing the flames on the other side of the car. So for now, here's a quick rundown of that process. Measure the area that the flames will go on, then it's back to the computer. I use Photoshop to resize the flame area of my drawing to the full-size measurements and then print it out. As the design area is larger than a single piece of paper, it takes a number of pages to print it out. These pages are taped together and I fit the pattern to the car to recheck the size. Then, using a light box or window, the reverse side of the pattern is traced in pencil. The drawing is then flipped over and taped to the car. The lines of the design are traced with a pencil and the design is transferred in this way to the surface of the car. Now I can follow these lines and use them as a reference when I tape off the design.

Be sure to tape around the edges of the panels. Cut the fineline tape and very thoroughly use masking tape to tape around the panel edges. Don't take shortcuts as you'll end up removing overspray that has snuck past the fineline. It will happen. So carefully check during the process for overspray.

When painting ghost flames, especially on light colors like white, the surface has to be flawless. No boogers, no bugs, no specs of colored dust, nothing. When painting flames or any graphic, most of the time the design area will be receiving several layers of paint, and while it's never a good idea to paint over noticeable flaws, small stuff can sometimes disappear under the new layers. But very little paint goes on when applying any kind of ghost image. If there is something that was missed and will show up, it must be repaired.

If the base coat is a solid color, then the repair is easy. Simply spray on more base color to cover the flaw. If it is a pearl or candy color, then it's something that has to be judged on a case by case basis. Pearl colors can sometimes be repaired by airbrushing some base coat and some pearl. Same thing goes for candy colors, but many times House of Kolor Candy Basecoats can be used to remedy this very thing.

I use Uncle Bill's Sliver Grippers to handle the ends of the tape. Most of the time I find I want to realign or rework the flame line, so the tape has to be moved. It's easier to grab the tape end with the tweezers than trying to grab it with your fingers or a stencil knife.

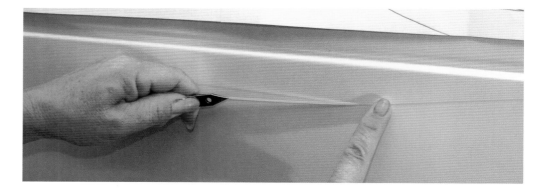

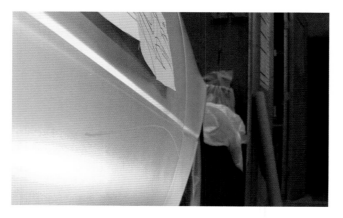

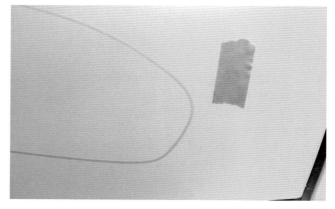

Above left: Sight down the flame lines to check and see how even the tape line is. This way, you can check for bumps in the lines. If the line is not smooth, grab the end of the tape with the tweezers, lift the tape off the surface, and rerun the tape line. **Above right:** What should you do if a curve isn't round and perfect? Here I've taped a curve that is too square.

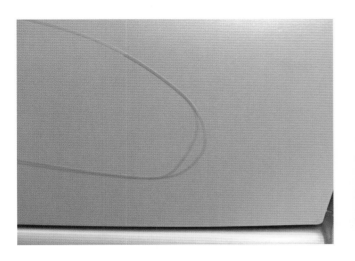
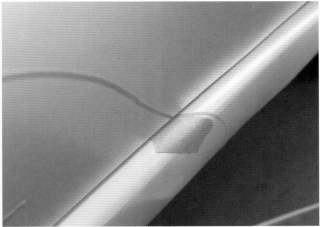

Above left: *I run another piece of fineline tape outside of the first curve, extending the curve and giving it an even, round shape.* **Above right:** *Oops! Here's a piece of tape that is not too straight. See the bend in the tape?*

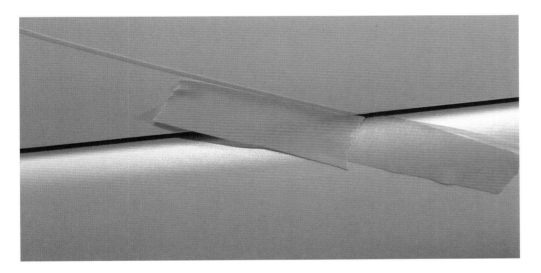

Left: *First I run either fineline or masking tape to reference where the tape goes. This way I don't lose the location. Then I pull up the flame fineline and rerun it. This time I lay it down so the flame outline is even, no bumps.* **Below left:** *This next step can be done by several methods. Each has its advantages and disadvantages. Either transfer tape or regular masking tape can be used. Using transfer tape is faster but it involves cutting into the fineline tape. Press too hard with the knife and you'll go right through to the paint surface and maybe leave a cut mark. Here I'm using masking tape because there's not much flame area, so it will not take long to mask these flames. The color is light. It will easily show flaws such as cut marks. At the end of the chapter I'll go through the other methods I use to mask off flames. Here, I start off with the ¾-inch tape overlapping the fineline tape and running it around the flames. I'll use ½-inch masking tape or narrower for tight areas, like between the flame licks and 2-inch tape for larger areas.*

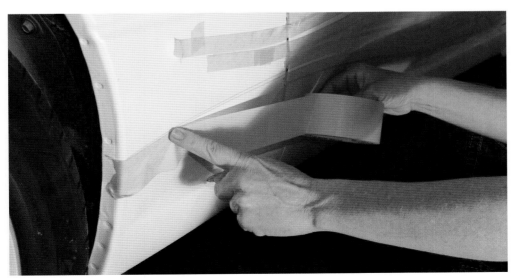

Top: *Try to use methods that save time. Sometimes this involves using materials that cost more money. Like 2-inch masking tape to quickly tape off oddly shaped areas. What good is it to save on materials if it takes longer to do the job? And always check your tape edges after you lay them out, to make sure the tape isn't puckering up or lifting on the edges. I use my fingernail to burnish down any lifting or bubbling tape edges. The other thing to watch for is tiny little spaces that haven't been covered by tape. I take two breaks away from my work while laying out flames. The second break is taken after the flame is taped off. When you go back to look at it, you'll find lots of small areas that paint will sneak through. The technique of taping off flames seen here can be used for painting flames other than ghost flames, like traditional (or hot rod) and airbrushed flames. So read through it and take notice of the many handy hints that will help in a pain-free flame job.* **Middle:** *Now to get the other side of the car taped off. This is where a pattern would have come in very handy. Since the design is traced on both sides in pencil, simply flip it over, line it up, tape it on, and trace along the lines. Now there will be an exact copy of the reversed design. But I can't do that here. So I flip over my reference drawing, put it on a light table or against a window and trace it. Now I have a reversed flame drawing to refer to as I tape the opposite side. I just hang it over the area I'm flaming and start to tape. After the taping is done look for any dark spots or flaws in the paint surface and if possible damp sand those away. Refer to the previous sidebar for more information.* **Bottom:** *Now get out the airbrushes. Make sure they are clean! One little bit of old dried paint blowing out of the airbrush will have you back at the previous step. I'll use House of Kolor PBC-57 Light Teal Pearl for the first layer of flames. I'll reduce it way down, about 200 percent. I always test a small place that the masking can be easy peeled back from. This is so I can check it to make sure the paint is not too heavy or too light. Too heavy, and the ghost effect is lost. Too light, and it can't be seen. The trick is to find the right balance of paint reduction and airbrush movement. A smart idea would be to do a test panel first, to see just how much paint you need to be airbrushing and how fast you need to move the airbrush. If you are doing ghost flames for the first time, do the test panel to gain some experience. Now with your airbrush at low pressure, maybe 15 psi, very lightly spray the edges of the tape in one spot. Then check it. One quick pass with the airbrush is all I use.*

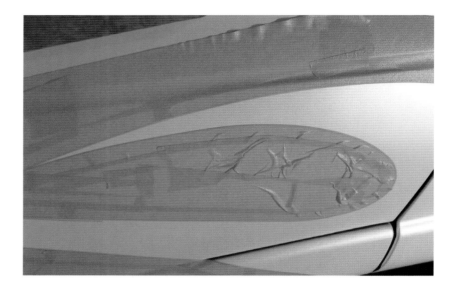

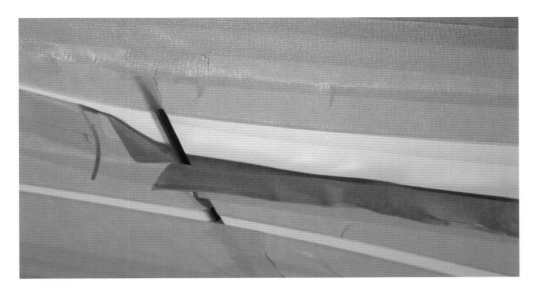

But I am not happy with it. I peel back the tape. The blue pearl has to be sprayed on so light that it looks pastel. This sports car needs evil attitude, not soft pastel colors. My original idea won't work. I remove all the tape and masking from where blue was sprayed and carefully wet sand the blue away with 800. I take care not to sand through the clearcoat into the pearl base.

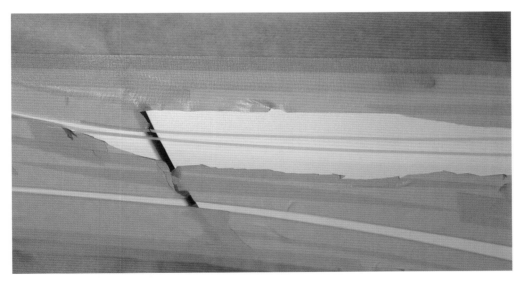

Once the blue is sanded off, the flame is taped off again.

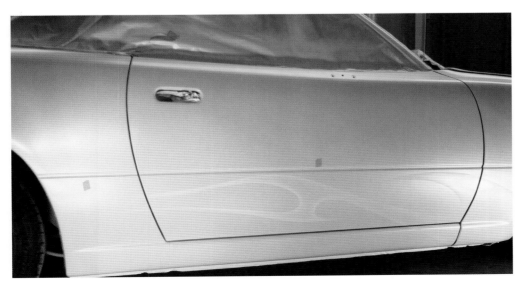

I consult with the customer and we decide to try and see what solid white would look like. It sure sounds like it will be perfect. White base coat is reduced down about 200 percent and very lightly airbrushed. The stark solid white softly contrasting against the glowing white pearl. And sure enough, it does. It's ghostly. It's perfect. Here's the first layer!

I go ahead and tape off the next and final layer. Then mask off and spray it.

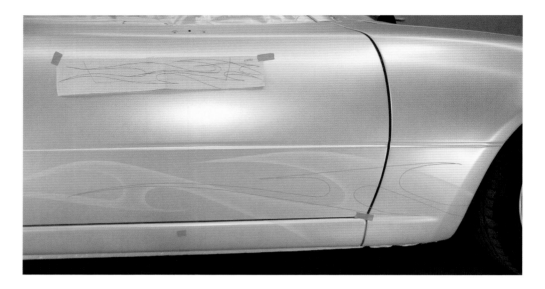

I move to the other side to spray and realize I haven't applied all the masking materials. But as I'm using very little paint at very light pressure and the color is so similar, that I don't need to mask that extensively. I use a technique where the tape is bent back, forming a "spraybreak." The overspray from the airbrush is directed away.

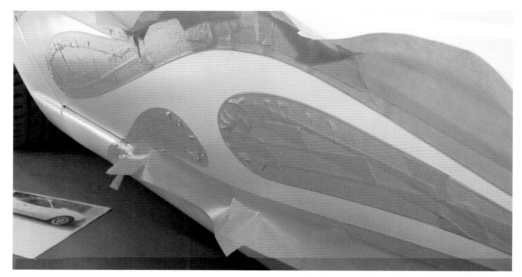

Next the masking materials are carefully removed, leaving the fineline tape in place. Always pull the tape away from itself. Since the paint is so thin, it dries very fast. I'll wait 15 minutes. But with any other kind of flame, you should pull up the tape a little and see if it breaks cleanly away. If it doesn't, then wait some more.

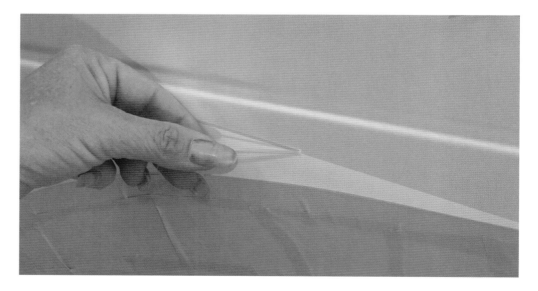

Here are the flames are done. They came out great. Not too noticeable, but when the light hits the car right, Wow! It's harder than it seems, but once a painter gets used to doing ghost effects, they can be the perfect artwork answer for vehicles that need some kind of design but not too much. See Chapter 14 for clear coat information.

HANDY HINTS

What should you do if the paint was applied very thickly, and no matter how long you wait or what you do, removing the tape does not leave a clean edge? Leave the tape in place. With a very sharp stencil knife like an X-Acto Number 11 or Number 4, carefully run the very point of the knife along the tape edge, cutting the excess paint away. Then remove the tape.

ALMOST-GHOST, MULTI-LAYER FLAMES

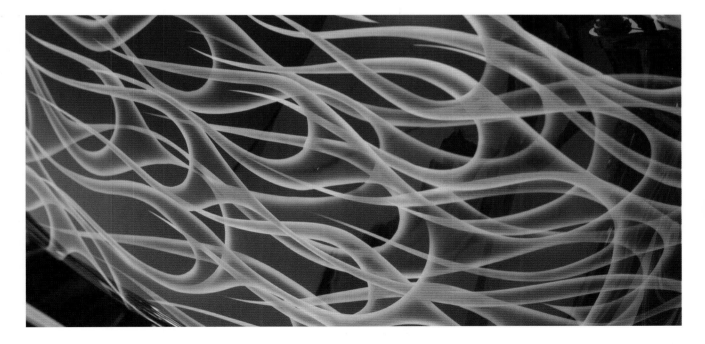

These flames aren't solid, but have too much color on them to be true ghost flames. Because of this, they can be done on solid colors or any color using solid colors. It's more of an effect between a real flame and a traditional flame. What I've done here is apply four coats of MetalFlake Company's Spray Mask. Using 1/16-inch fineline tape, lay out a flame, then cut along the edges, and peel out the material. Using a yellow/white mix base coat heavily reduced, lightly spray along the edges. Next spray the inside of the flame with candy orange concentrate or dye mixed with base coat clear. Repeat, only tape off parts of the first flame that don't cross into the new one. Keep repeating the process until all the layers are done.

TRADITIONAL FLAMES USING SILVER LEAF

There must be a hundred books that talk about painting flames. So this next step-by-step will be short but meaty. I'm applying flames to a Mini hood, which already has a skull painted on it. These flames will be done in a traditional technique, but with a nontraditional method. Metal leaf comes in several varieties, better known as gold leaf (which is actual gold), silver leaf, and metal leaf which comes in various colors such as green, black, blue and red.

"Metal leaf is some tedious stuff. How do you handle it without it breaking apart?" I hear this from painters all the time. But with a little patience and a little knowledge, doing metal leaf work can be fun. I really like working with it. I like to use silver leaf under candy paint. For this step-by-step I'm applying silver leaf.

Next I gather up the stuff I'll need to do the leaf work. From left to right, clockwise: Silver leaf, adhesive size, squirrel hair lettering brush, House of Kolor AP-01 Adhesive Promoter, transfer tape, masking tape, 1/16-inch green fineline tape, scissors, Xacto #4 stencil knife, and piece of velvet. I'll also need a pad of tracing paper.

The flames are taped off using 1/16-inch green fineline tape.

HANDY HINT
There is good quality silver leaf and not so good. If you cannot look at the actual sheet of leaf before purchasing, only buy one book of leaf and check it out. You want the leaf surface to have a real shiny sheen to it. Poor quality silver leaf has a dull sheen to it. This is also true of gold leaf, but not as critical. Look for a soft, shiny glow.

GHOST FLAMES AND SILVER LEAF FLAMES

114

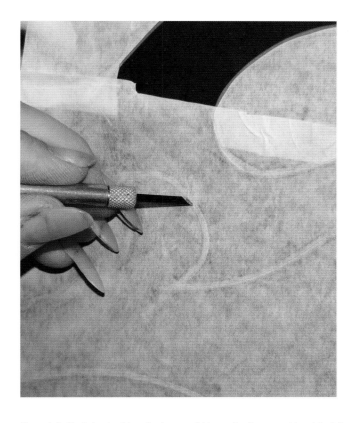

Above left: *Next sheets of transfer tape are laid over the flames and burnished down on each side of the tape. Using a Number 4 Xacto knife, I cut on top of the tape and trim away and material that hangs into the flame area (note the left side of the hood). Take care not to cut through the fineline into the paint surface, as it will leave cut marks. If trying this for the first time, stop and check to see just how deeply you're cutting. Using the tweezers, lift a small portion of the tape layers up and see if the cuts go through into the paint layers. If so, then simply use less pressure. It's a matter of gaining experience to know how much pressure to apply when cutting. Then the rest of the hood is masked off with paper.* **Above right:** *A thin, even layer of size is brushed on. Make sure the brush is very clean. Then wash the brush immediately in soapy water. As the adhesive dries, it will change from a milky white to clear. When it is completely clear it is ready for leaf application. Sometimes it takes an hour, but the shop was hot the day I did this job and it dried in 15 minutes.*

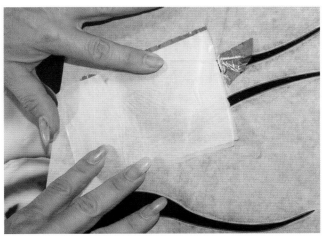

Above left: *The leaf tears very easily. So I sandwich a sheet of leaf in between two pieces of tracing paper and cut it into strips that will fit the space where it will be put.* **Above right:** *Now here's the tricky part. I hold up the leaf above where it will be placed, let the bottom sheet of paper drop away, and place the leaf onto the surface. If you have a fan in your shop, make sure it's off. Any movement of air will blow the leaf sheet around.*

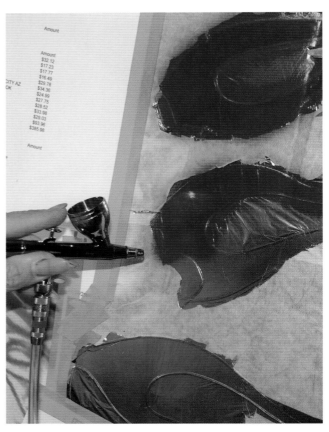

Above left: *Smooth the leaf on the design surface by softly smoothing the tracing paper on the leaf. Don't press too hard. It tears very easy. Use a fingernail to burnish the leaf into the corners up against the tape edge. You may want to use a piece of velvet to smooth the surface and burnish the leaf onto the surface. I always start out working on top of the tracing paper. Then I wrap a piece of velvet cloth around a fingertip and gently but firmly smooth down the leaf. Keep smoothing back and forth until the surface looks very metal-like and very flat. If the leaf crumples against the sized surface, just pull off the leaf that didn't stick, and carefully lay strips of leaf around what is there. Don't lose patience with this process. Once you get the hang of handling the leaf, it's a breeze.* **Above right:** *There will be places where the leaf will overlap itself. Make sure the extra leaf in those areas is removed by brushing the extra leaf away with your very clean fingers. Don't heavily touch the leaf! Closely look over the surface and make sure all the loose bits of leaf are wiped away. This is very important. Bubbles can form under loose leaf, so go over the surface carefully. For any areas where the leaf came off, simply dab some size on and apply more leaf. Now with the airbrush, apply two light coats of House of Kolor AP-10 Adhesion Promoter, applied only over the leaf area. Don't skip this step, or the paint may not stick to the leaf. I still have more paint going on over the leaf, but at this point, if no further paintwork will be done on the leaf, clear coat should be applied. If you're working over base coat clear, use base coat clear. If working over urethane clear, use that. Do not use base coat clear over urethane, as that can, in some cases, result in adhesion problems. Here I've sprayed the AP-01 and I'm now spraying two coats of House of Kolor Candy Brandywine.*

If this is your first time doing leaf work, please do a test piece first. Different brands of paint react in different ways, so play around, and make sure the paint sticks to the leaf. This is why when you're trying a new technique, you should do a test piece first so you can get used to the materials.

HANDY HINT
Once the tape is removed, what if any size has snuck past the tape? This is carefully wiped off with precleaner and a folded paper towel. Don't touch the leaf.

HANDY HINT
To get that classic effect when doing real gold leaf, stick a wad of fabric onto the end of a stick. Then wrap a piece of velvet around the wad, securing it with tape around the handle. Now put the velvet pad against the surface of the leaf and give it a gentle turn. Move it over a bit and do it again. Keep repeating along the surface of the leaf, creating soft swirls. Do this before the tape or stencil is removed.

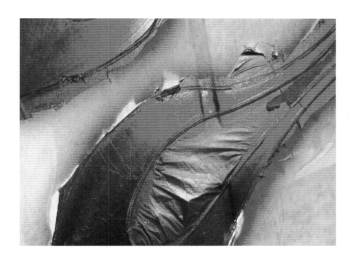

Above: *The flames really have a great red glow to them. The leaf reflects the light as if chrome were under the red candy. The flames are done.* **Above right:** *Here's the finished hood with clear coat applied. The flames painted in this chapter did not need to be pinstriped. But most of time flames need to be striped with a flawless, thin, smooth line. I usually take flamed parts to someone who can freehand stripe as good as I can airbrush. See Chapter 13 for more information on pinstriping.*

MULTI-LAYERED AIRBRUSHED FLAMES

Here's an example of airbrushed flames done in a fade. Very simply stated, a double or multi-layer flame technique is just like any other flame style except more sets of flames are added. And in order to give them a truly 3D effect, parts of each set must be taped off in order for the flames to overlap and intertwine. Pick the flame parts that will be overlapped and tape them off. The example seen here starts with the airbrush concentrated on the center portions of the flame, spraying as little material as possible along the edges. This will result in less paint edge and lesser chance of the problem of a lighter undercoat peeking out around the edges of the flames. Now that wouldn't be a big problem if the flames were pinstriped, but here they are not. Then take a darker candy color and spray along the edge of the flames, softly fading the color toward the middle of the flame. Where the flames overlap, add a light black shadow using a very reduced black. I find a soft shadow is more effective than a dark one. See Chapter 10 for more details on painting multilayer artwork.

MISCELLANEOUS FLAME "TIPS"

After the flames have dried, but not so dry that the edge flakes, use the sliver tweezers and remove any taping material. Always pull any flame taping material in the opposite direction, back and away from how it is laid down. Carefully brush away any loose paint edges with your clean finger and softly wet sand the areas that are not flamed with 800-grit to remove any paint that has snuck past the tape. If using Spray Mask to mask the flame, this step will remove any impressions from the tape that bordered the Spray Mask.

Try not to get too thick a paint edge with your flames. I tend to airbrush my flames with most of the color concentrated toward the middle of the flame. If I'm doing a faded flame, with darker colors airbrushed around the edges, I spray the middle with the lighter colors, allowing the color to fade near the edge. Then I go over the edges with the darker color.

A shadow softly airbrushed under the flame will add a 3D effect. Simply tape off the bottom edge of the flame and use a thinned-down black to spray a soft shadow. Just enough shadow. Not too dark.

In the event there is a very heavy paint edge, look at it closely. If it sticks up too high, a flap of paint may have formed. This will need to be trimmed away with a very sharp razor blade. Just lay the blade edge flat on the surface and softly trim the edge down. If this flap is painted over, an air pocket may form which will result in a bubble under the paint. Don't worry if you mess up the edge of the flame. You can always go back after the first round of clear coat, tape off that edge, and retouch it with the airbrush. In fact, that's what I do a lot. I have to go back and redo a few lines here and there on most of my jobs. It's no biggie, so don't sweat it if you see mistakes.

When shading the edges of airbrushed flames, sometimes overspray from the darker color can land and settle in the center of the flame and cause a mottled effect. To help combat this, before shading the flame, spray some base coat or intercoat clear over the flame center prior to edging them.

Now you'll notice that on the surface at the places where the tape was run, you can see impressions of the tape. What I do is I lightly wet sand the entire area that was not flamed with 800- or 1,000-grit, removing these lines and any other overspray or foreign objects that have settled onto the surface.

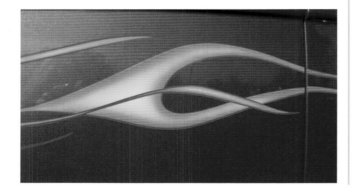

Left: Close-up of a metal effect tribal flame done with Spray Mask. Using Spray Mask as the stencil helped to get the sharp curves the tribal design required.

Below: This color combination of purple and blue gets a lot of compliments. What I did was airbrush the flame first with a light base coat of the finished color. Light blue base for the blue flame. Then blue candy was faded in around the edges. Next the whole flame was coated with candy. Take care not to mix the candy too darkly or too thick or else the fade will be grainy. Make sure to wait until the lower flame layer is dry before the next layer is masked off.

CHAPTER 10
EVIL GRAPHICS ON A FORD EXPLORER

In this chapter I will go over techniques that can be used not only with graphics but also with any kind of custom artwork, like flames or lettering. I'll profile how to use the airbrush to give form and boldness, using pearl paint, and trying something new with a spatter effect.

Left: *The Crazy Horse shop truck gives no clue that the driver is a custom painter. My friends have been giving me grief about my plain-Jane white Ford Explorer ever since I bought it seven years ago. It didn't bother me then. It was my shop truck and it was nice to blend in with all the other anonymous white SUVs. Twenty years ago there were towns I couldn't even drive through because my 1966 Mustang was so noticeable, all evil sounding with wide tires. I was just asking to be pulled over.* **Below:** *First off, I have to design a paint job. Somehow I just can't picture this truck with flames. I've always liked the California style of graphics: multiple layers of bright, wicked color slicing across the side of a truck or car. I make a few copies of the truck photo. Then I begin to sketch until I come up with something I like. Now I'll make a half-dozen copies of that. These will be blanks.*

EQUIPMENT AND MATERIAL

Prismacolor pencils
Lead pencil
⅛-inch, ½-inch, ¾-inch, and 2-inch masking tape
⅛-inch and ¹⁄₁₆-inch green fineline tape
Masking paper
Eraser
Yellow base coat
White base coat
Blue base coat
House of Kolor SG-100 Intercoat Clear
House of Kolor PBC65 Passion Pearl
House of Kolor KK12 Pagan Gold Kandy Koncentrate
House of Kolor KK08 Tangerine Kandy Koncentrate
House of Kolor KK17 Violette Kandy Koncentrate
House of Kolor KK18 Pink Kandy Koncentrate
House of Kolor KK04 Oriental Blue Kandy Koncentrate

House of Kolor RU Reducer
House of Kolor UC-35 Kosmic Klear Urethane
Gerson Blend prep tack cloths
Gerson tack rag
EZ-Mix cups
Coast Airbrush's solvent-proof mixing bottles
Gray Scotchbrite pad
600- and 800-grit wet sand paper
Magnets
SATAjet 2000 HVLP digital spray gun
SATAminijet 3 spray gun
SATAminijet 4 spray gun
SATA dekor 2000 artbrush
Iwata HP-C airbrush
Uncle Bill's Sliver Gripper tweezers

Where do I get ideas? I used to wonder where great custom painters came up with their wild designs. Sometimes I know right away what I envision the design to be. It has to complement the vehicle and make the most of the vehicle's lines. As this truck is pretty boxy, I want to keep the design down low, stretch out the truck, give it some zip, and wake it up. Many times, I'll go through magazines and files to get ideas. I even have an idea folder where I keep designs I came up with but never used. I'll lay all my ideas out in front of me, then get out my colored pencils and start drawing and coloring.

HANDY HINT

One thing to always consider when custom painting trucks is the amount of area being worked on. Everything is big. It will take quite a bit of urethane clear to clear this entire truck. That can translate into hundreds of dollars of material. Keep that in mind when quoting prices for custom painting any vehicle. Or, if you're new at custom painting, remember to figure clear coat material into the costs. There'll be clear coat for filling over artwork. Then there will be more clear for final finishing.

It's not just the artwork that will eat up hours. There are situations when prep sanding and taping will take as much time as the artwork itself. Be honest with yourself and save your sanity later by being realistic about exactly what any custom paint project will require in actual work hours and material costs.

These "blanks" are great for trying out color choices. For all your years spent with coloring books, this is the adult version. The first one doesn't do anything for me. The dark purple keeps it toned down too much. The second version is very bright—too bright. This would look great on a motorcycle or a hot rod truck, but it's too much for the Explorer. The last one is perfect. I'm not a big fan of yellow, but it works here. And it's late—I need a design. Actually, I really do like this one.

HANDY HINT

Many painters use projectors to get an image on the side of a truck or car. This is great if the lights can be turned down low or if it's dark out. If you're used to using a projector and you want to reverse a drawing for the other side of the vehicle, simply load the drawing into your computer, reverse (or flip) it horizontally, print it out, and slap on the projector plate.

This next little trick looks like more of a pain than it is. First I pick a measurement in the design area. Here I'll get a measurement from the back of the front wheelwell to the front of the rear wheelwell. Then I scan the drawing into my computer. Using a graphics program (in this case Photoshop, but others will work) I crop the drawing so only the graphic I drew remains. The measurement I took was from the front of the graphic to the very back, the orange tip that touches the rear wheelwell. Now I'll bring up the resizing or "Image Size" feature. One of the boxes in the pop-up window will allow me to resize the cropped drawing in inches. I resize the drawing to 73 inches long, making sure that the proportions box is checked. This way, the width will be readjusted to match. Now I print it out. I'll get a whole bunch of pages that I will have to tape together. But now I have a true-sized pattern for the design. I trim away any excess and tape it in place on the truck.

I can step back and see that this design will work. As I'll be removing the pattern and then placing it up again, I use tape and make marks that will help me align the drawing again. Note how the drawing has a line on it right where the door ends and the quarter panel starts.

Now the pattern is taped back onto the truck. I simply line up the edge of the drawing with the tape I put down and line up the marks. I use magnets to hold the drawing in place. Then I trace along the lines of design. The pencil material on the back side of the paper is transferred to the surface of the truck, and my design is ready to be taped off.

First I tape off the design area, running masking tape and masking paper along the black trim that frames the area. Using 1/8-inch green fineline tape, the design is taped off. First I tape up the yellow "Z" layer. I tape the pattern above the area so I can easily refer to it if I need to.

The drawing flipped over and taped over a window. Now I'll trace against all the lines with a pencil.

The design is completely masked off. I use a combination of masking paper and plastic. You can see where I used magnets to hold the paper and plastic down.

Using a pink eraser, remove any pencil marks straying into the design area. While it may seem like paint would cover any such marks, you don't want a heavy buildup of paint. Also, many lighter colors such as white, blue, or any light color will show marks through a couple of coats of paint. Yellow is especially prone to this.

HANDY HINT

More is not better when it come to paint thickness. Try to keep the paint thickness down. A thicker paint edge means more clear will be needed to level out the surface. This means more drying time and more hassle. And sanding can be a nightmare, as it's easy to quickly sand through the clear into the edge and reveal a different color that was under that particular layer of paint. And don't flood the paint around the edges. When things are taped off, it can look like more paint needs to be applied, when in fact there is plenty already there. Less paint thickness means quicker drying times, which means the painter can mask off layers quicker and get the job done quicker. And less filler clear is used, so both time and material are saved.

Above left: *Now is the time to tack rag and blow off any debris or dust on the surface. Any raised areas, such as a bit of dust that gets painted over, will create a shadow once the candy shading is applied. The candy overspray will hit it and create a dark spot. Using my SATAminijet 3, I spray on two coats of yellow base coat.* **Above right:** *Here's the extremely high-tech setup I used for my airbrushes. I take a table and simply tape my airbrush holders to the edge. It easily holds my airbrushes. Plus, the SATA artbrush has its own holder that keeps it ready for use. I tend the make my setups from what is around. I'll tape airbrush holders to anything.*

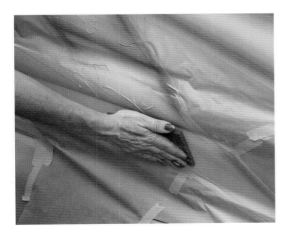

Now here's where it gets tricky. While it may seem easy enough to airbrush candy shading, it can be tricky. The candy must be applied very evenly or it will appear blotchy. As you try to correct the blotchiness, more paint is applied, and then it gets too dark. Then it must be lightened up and reshaded, so take your time when doing the shading. Start soft. You can always add more. Another way to help keep the shading even is to mix the paint on the "light" side. I mix all my own candies. I'll mix House of Kolor Kandy Koncentrate into HOK SG-100 Intercoat Clear. Here I mix in some KK08 Tangerine. As for how much to mix in, I do it by eye. Just drizzle some tangerine into the clear, not too light, not too dark. Lighter is better than darker. I then will pour off some of the mixture and add more reducer to thin it further. I'll start off with the thinner mix. I want the shading to be very even and gradual. One way to keep those dark spots from happening is to lightly go over the area with a gray Scotch-Brite pad, removing any dust that got caught in the previously applied base coat. (Note: This cannot be done if the base coat was a metallic or pearl, as the scratches will show.)

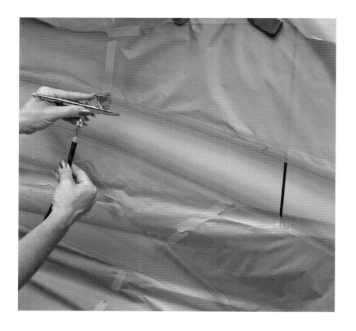

Using an Iwata HP-C, I'll lightly spray the tangerine along the edges of the yellow, feathering it into the middle. Next I do the same thing with the Pagan Gold Mixture, only extending even further into the yellow. Once I have the gradual tones down, I'll load the airbrush with the darker mixture of tangerine. This will be applied right along the edges, giving them a nice dark shadow. Make sure the mixture isn't too thick or has too much color, because it will look uneven. If that happens, simply airbrush yellow down the center and feather it toward the edges. Then thin down the color used for shading and apply again.

HANDY HINT

An easy way to check any paint mixture you're using for shading is to spray a little on the masking paper. If it appears grainy or spotty, then it is too dark or too thick. Either add more clear and reducer or just add reducer. Experience will let you know which one to add, so don't rush if you are new at this. Take your time.

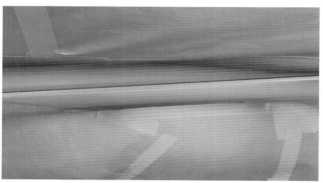

Above left: Now here's something to watch for! See how the edge of this trim has picked up color? As it is in the center of the stripe, it should have yellow in the middle of the stripe area. But tangerine has landed there. What happens is that any kind of raised edge will catch overspray, the same thing that happens when overspray catches a piece of dust in the paint. This tends to happen with any body line. In fact, as there is this piece of trim running down the center of the artwork area, as well as a body crease line below it, I will have to watch carefully as I go through this artwork process and rework these areas. **Above right:** And here's the way it's fixed. I simply airbrush the base color through the middle of the section. In this case, it's yellow. As I need the repair to be soft and to blend well, I check to make sure the yellow is not too thick. I spray some on the masking paper next to the area, and find it's perfect. The orange overspray is covered with only a few strokes of the airbrush.

The masking materials are removed, and the yellow slash is revealed. It turned out more orange than the drawing. I may go back later and "yellow" it up. But for now I leave it. Next, the purple, pink, and blue slashes are taped off with ⅛-inch green fineline tape. I prefer the green compared to the blue fineline tape. The blue bends around corners better, but the green is stiffer and it holds a straight line better. In fact, I would have preferred to use ¼-inch green fineline, but I was out of it and there was no time to have more delivered.

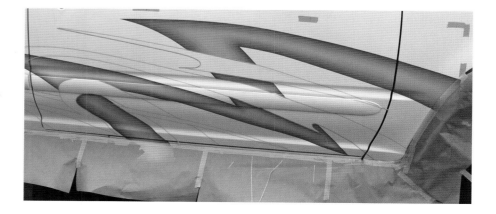

HANDY HINT

Check your materials before each job! You could be making do with what you have on hand, when it would be easier to use a different product! Or worse, you can't do the job at all. You may also find that a product you were going to use is no longer any good. You pick up that can of catalyst and find that it is a solid mass, rather than a liquid. So check your materials in advance.

All taped off and ready to spray. As I need to spray the different colors separately, I'll now tape off the blue and pink areas, leaving the purple areas exposed.

Left: *With my SATAminijet 3, I spray House of Kolor Passion Purple Pearl. As you can see from the photo, it is not mixed too thick. HOK recommends that their pearls be reduced down with two parts pearl to one part reducer, which is what I have done here.* **Below:** *I mix HOK KK17 Violette Kandy Koncentrate with some Intercoat Clear and airbrush that along the top edge of the slash. As the purple pearl base is so dark, I make sure the candy mix is dark enough, but not dark enough to spray grainy.*

HANDY HINT

Artwork processes can take months, sometimes years . . . well, it can feel like it at times. But they will take hours. And if your paint is sitting around for hours, reducer will evaporate out of it and it will get thicker. If you're keeping your paint in bottles, like Coast Airbrush's solvent-proof mixing bottles, then it's not much of a problem. But if you're using disposable cups and mixing as you go, which is what I was doing here, after an hour or so, the paint will get thicker. Keep this in mind and reduce accordingly. I tend to mix colors specific to a certain job, so I don't need to keep them when I'm done. And some colors don't store well for very long. They break down too fast, so I don't waste a storage bottle for those.

Above left: *I wait for a while until the purple is dry enough to tape off, maybe 15 minutes, because I kept my paint thickness low. The area for the pink slash is untaped, and the purple is now taped off. I mix HOK KK18 Pink Kandy Koncentrate into some Intercoat Clear. I'll spray some white base coat down first to ensure that the candy mix sticks to the very hard factory finish on my truck. Then I airbrush the pink candy mix over that, airbrushing more candy along the top edge to get that dark edge, which I'm hoping creates the illusion of a three-dimensional shadow.* **Above right:** *Now the pink is allowed to dry. I wait another 15 minutes and see that it is dry enough to tape. I untape the area for the blue slash and tape up the pink. I mix up some blue base coat and spray that on with my minijet 3. I'm using a minigun rather than an airbrush, as I want the paint surface to be smooth and even, and airbrushes don't work as well for large areas. Now I want to try something different. I want to get a spatter effect on the blue. I'd like to use a lighter blue and a teal spatter. I add some white base coat to my blue to lighten it up and I do not reduce it! For teal, I'll add a bit of green toner to my blue mix. I pour the glop of unreduced paint into my SATAjet 2000 spray gun. I have a large-sized WSB nozzle and needle set on this gun. I'll need that in order for the thick paint to come out. Actually, I'd like to go bigger, but I don't have a larger nozzle set on hand, and this was a last-minute decision. I keep my air pressure as low as possible, about 10 psi at the gun, and hold the gun so the paint literally "falls" onto the surface.*

HANDY HINT

Cobwebbing is a cool effect that lays down strands of unreduced paint. Spatter effect is similar but it gives more of a spatter of paint bits than whole strands. Either effect can be very cool. But the one thing you will need for these effects, other than unreduced paint and low air pressure, is a gun with a large nozzle, preferably a 1.7 or larger. In addition, gravity feed guns break up the paint too well to effectively cobweb. A siphon feed gun should be used. And as this stuff will go everywhere, make sure the floor is covered beneath the vehicle as you'll end up with a paint-spattered floor. That may look cool, but that's where you'll be stepping, and you'll end up with paint footsteps all over the shop.

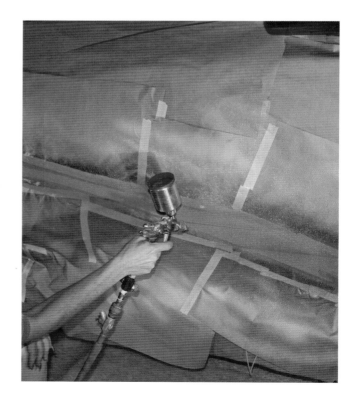

Now, since I'm making this up as I go along, I decide to do several layers of spatter. With my trusty SATAminijet 4, I spray on a coat of Intercoat Clear mixed with a little HOK KK04 Oriental Blue Kandy Koncentrate. Then I'll airbrush more blue candy mix along the top edge of the slash to create that shadowed top edge.

Next I'll spatter paint the light blue and then the teal base coat over that, but not too heavily. Actually, I spray it sparingly. Just enough to see the two different colors of spatter. Here's a close-up. Note the dark top edge.

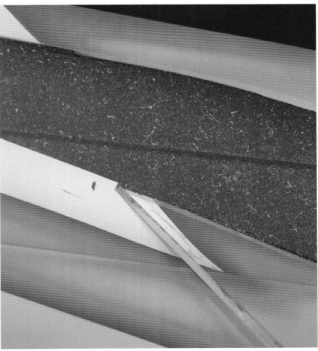

Yeah! It's time to peel off the masking materials! First I peel back the masking tape and paper, leaving the fineline tape in place. I do this because the paint is still kind of soft and not hard yet. It wouldn't take much to mess up that paint edge. I always pull back, never up, on any masking tape, as I want the tape to break the paint edge.

Now I pull back the fineline tape. Again, pulling it back against itself, cleanly breaking the paint edge. Note the bit of blue paint that snuck past the tape? There are a few of these. What I'll do is go back with wet 800 sanding paper and wet sand away any kind of pencil line, debris, and overspray that remains on the white surface.

OK, here's what I have so far. Now for the next step, the teal background.

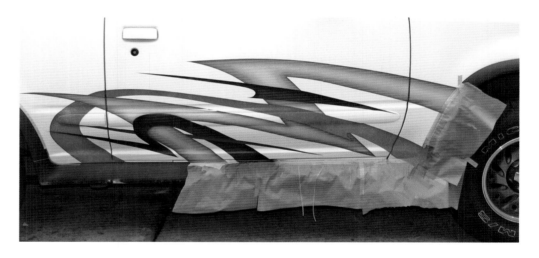

Some painters would have sprayed the background first. But I wanted to get started quickly, and there is always the possibility of the newly applied base causing problems with the other artwork layers, such as darker candies bleeding through lighter colors. The teal shading I used on the background could bleed through the yellow slash. Besides, I still would have had to go back and spray shadows under the graphics. So I'm doing it this way. I have to tape off all the layers I just finished. I let the layers dry overnight and then, using ½-inch, ¾-inch, and 2-inch masking tapes, the layers are carefully taped off. For the taped ends, I'll trim ⅛-inch fineline tape to cover the sharp points. Taping off these layers on one side takes me about an hour. You can do the background either way, spray them before the top layers or after. Each way has its pros and cons. I also liked the fact that the white factory finish was easy to work over, and it gave my layers a glow, as the color lit up when applied over a white. Plus, I would have had to use more paint in my layers, as I would have had to apply white to cover up the teal background.

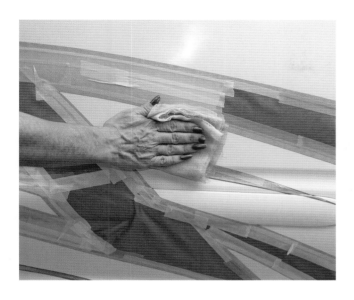

Above left: *The background is now ready to be sprayed and carefully tacked and blown off to remove any debris.* **Above right:** *I mix some teal toner into my base coat white. I want the background to have a teal tone, but as I'll be airbrushing teal candy mix on it, I want it to be light. It's nearly as light as the white factory paint. I only apply the teal base in the areas inside the layers. Not above them.*

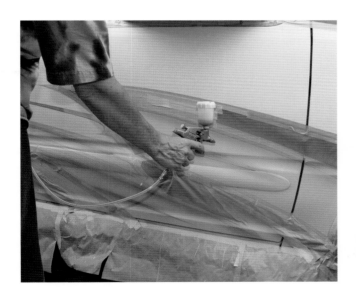

Above left: *With my SATA dekor 2000 artbrush, I begin the candy teal shading, running the shading along the bottom edges of the layers, creating shadow. Once again, my candy mix is not overly dark or thick. I want this to be very gradual. Please note: These pictures show the teal as being lighter than it actually is. In the pictures it shows up as a pastel tone, but actually it is much deeper and richer looking.* **Above right:** *Now I airbrush in more teal, building up the shadow under those layers.* **Left:** *With the dekor, I add more shading, creating even more transition between the teal base and the heavy shadow under the slashes. Watch to make sure the teal is not grainy, but even and soft. If it is grainy, add a little reducer.*

 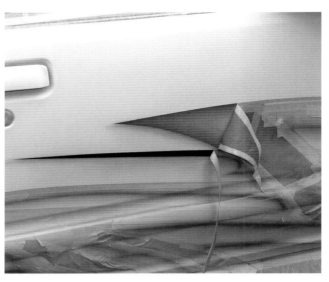

Above left: *Now I decide to add a little more interest. I load some teal base coat into my HP-C and airbrush a few light streaks across the teal.* **Above right:** *I need to check and see if I have the teal shading dark enough. Using my handy Sliver Gripper tweezers, I pull back two sections of the tape over the layers and see I need to darken up the shadow just under the slashes, plus extend the teal shading over the yellow slash. The transition between the graphic and the white basepaint is too harsh. It needs to be softened up.*

I make those changes and start to remove the tape from the slashes. But I find that the shadowing under the top purple slash is still not dark enough. I quickly tape it off. I run 2-inch masking tape and bend the top half, forming a "spray break." This will direct the overspray away from the white over it.

And here it is! All that needs to be done now is for the slashes to be pinstriped. For that, see Chapter 13. But first I'll apply about five coats of a filler urethane clear like HOK's UC-35 over the artwork. I apply the first coat lightly, as I did not use any Intercoat Clear over the artwork. The heavy weight of the urethane can grab the artwork paint and literally drag it down. It is allowed to dry and then wet sanded with 600.

The finished truck. What a difference the pinstripes make! Too bad the colors don't show as strongly in the photo. See Chapter 13 for close up photos.

Above left: *Ryan Young did this cool graphic on his shop wagon. It's a combination of pretty simple techniques. The orange was done by laying down a pearl orange base, the holding flame stencils over it, spraying candy orange, moving the stencil, spraying again and keep repeating. The gold/brown strip was taped off prior to painting the orange. Then it was masked off and a very thinned down black pearl was sprayed over a hand held mask with the technique used in spraying the orange candy. It's finished off with simple striping.* **Above right:** *Less is more many times with graphics. The rear section of the wagon graphic is sleek and elegant.*

One of my first "decent" truck graphic paint jobs. The truck is two toned. Then the area between the split is taped off eight inches below the dark top color. Four coats of Spray Mask were applied to that area. After it dried, the tribal graphic was drawn on and cut out. Then a contrasting dark maroon pearl was spayed on. The masking materials were removed and the tribal was striped with a bright orange.

I love painting tailgates. The same masking method was used for the tailgate. But here's the trick to getting each side of the design to match. When sketching out the design, I split the tailgate down the center and drew out the design on one side. Then I laid tracing paper over it, lining up the edge of the paper with the centerline, and traced the design on the paper. Next the paper was flipped over and placed on the other side of the tailgate, lining up the edge of the paper with the centerline. I traced on the design with a pen and the pencil lead on the back of the paper transferred the design to the surface.

CHAPTER 11
PAINTING SKULLS

I like painting skulls. There's something about working the bone texture to obtain different effects. Bone texture technique can widely vary. I have included a few photos of skull artwork I have done to show the many different effects that can be obtained. Read through the step-by-step, and then plan out your design and process. Don't rush through it. Chances are you'll achieve better results with your first skull flame paint than I did.

If you can't draw a skull, go online or to a bookstore and look up skull photos or drawings. First you need a skull template. It's easy to make one. I have gathered an extensive reference library of skull pictures over the years, and you can too. Anatomy books, like *Gray's Anatomy*, can be a big help. When I started painting skulls, I looked at the work of airbrush artists whose work I admired. I had a copy of *Gray's Anatomy* left over from art school that suddenly came in very handy. I looked at photos of skulls and took pictures of an actual human skull. I studied the way the light hits the bone and how it defines it. I have a few actual animal skulls and they are more brown or cream color than white. Many skulls are painted using warm colors with mixtures of brown, yellow, and red, along with the black and white, to get a more realistic skull. But my style tends toward a whiter skull.

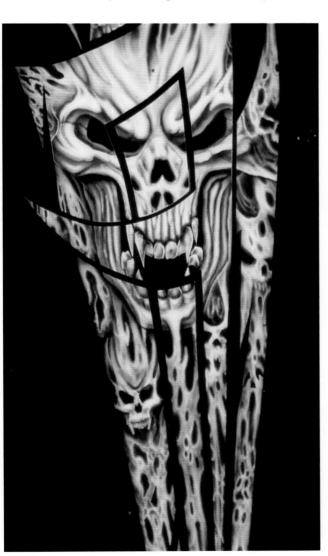

MATERIALS AND EQUIPMENT
Grafix frisket film
Roll of transfer tape
1/16-inch green fineline tape
TransferRite Ultra Transfer Tape
Masking tape
Base coat paint colors for skull
White
Black
Blue base tint
Base coat clear or Intercoat Clear
Fineline permanent marker pens such as
Pigma Micron 005
Sakura Microperm 01
Koh-I-Noor Rapidograph
(These are found only in artist supply stores.)
SATAgraph 3 airbrush
SATA dekor artbrush
Iwata HP-C airbrush
Iwata Micron C airbrush
Seamstress measuring tape (soft tape measure used in
   sewing)
Small magnets
Uncle Bill's Sliver Gripper tweezers
Light table or window
Soft lead pencil
Pink eraser
X-Acto Knife Number 4
X-Acto Knife Number 11
Drawing board

Don't just rush into mural artwork. Do your research. Go to a bookstore and find books with good pictures of the subject matter you are painting. Hopefully you'll be painting more of that subject and you'll be all set because you are building up a reference library. Whenever possible, work from photos of the subject matter. Slip a plastic sandwich bag over the photo to protect it from the paint overspray and tape it up close to what you are working on. Sometimes I tape a photo right to the tank or part I am working on, right next to where I am airbrushing.

Some companies, like Artool, sell skull templates that can be used to airbrush detailed large skulls or get ghostly soft skull effects, which can used as graphic effects to fill flames, panels, or other artwork areas.

The first thing is to draw up a skull. Another trick is to load the photo or drawing into your computer and use a graphics program to stretch the skull in different directions. Here I've drawn up a skull, and then used my copier to enlarge it. As the enlarged drawing is bigger than a single sheet of paper, I reposition the original drawing on the scanner bed and make the enlarged copy. Then using a light box or window, line up the lines of the drawing and tape the copies together. I like to use this to check the size of the skull on the part itself. Next I'll cut it out.

Next the skull is checked for size on the surface to be painted. Looks to be the right size.

Now, if I were doing this on the sides of a vehicle, I would flip the template over and trace the skull again on another piece of frisket paper, creating a matching reverse stencil. This would be used on the opposite side. Now if I had not been so cheap and had a plotter, I could have cut out a vinyl stencil from the drawing, and used that. Next I'll lay the stencil around the cut-out drawing on the hood.

Use a light table to trace the enlarged drawing. If you don't have a light table, tape the template to a window (you must do this during the day), then tape some frisket paper over it and trace away. I use Grafix frisket film. It's got a matte finish, so it's easy to draw on, and it's low tack. All frisket papers are not alike. Some use a cheap adhesive and leave residue. Using a Number 4 X-Acto knife, I cut out the skulls. I use a drawing board with a thin piece of cardboard on it for a cutting surface.

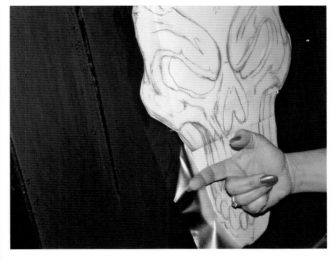

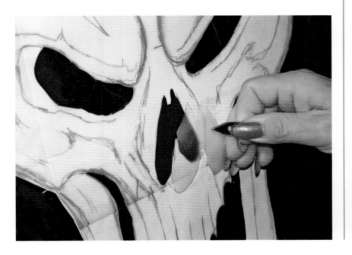

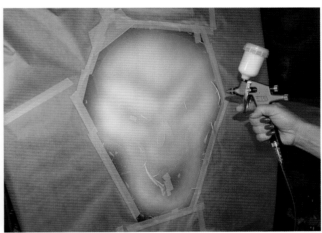

Above left: *Now the eye sockets and nose are cut out of the drawing and frisket cutouts are inserted in those areas. I use the Sliver Gripper tweezers to handle those pieces. At this time I start making paper copies of the enlarged drawing. These will be used for hand-held stencils to get sharp detail in individual areas, like the around the eye sockets and cheekbones.* **Above right:** *The rest of the hood is masked off. I tend to overreduce the colors I used when painting skulls. I like for the undertones to reflect through the upper layers. This helps create a three-dimensional effect. I mix up some white base coat and spray a somewhat light coat onto the skull, using my SATA dekor artbrush.*

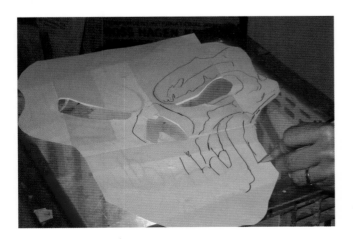

Now I flip the enlarged drawing over and, using a window or light table, I trace along the lines with a lead pencil. Then the drawing is placed over the open area of the skull and lined up.

HANDY HINT
I prefer mechanical lead pencils over regular pencils. No need to sharpen. But if I need a very sharp end on the lead of my mechanical pencil, I simply roll the lead around back and forth on paper to create a nice sharp point.

Using a pen, I trace along the lines. The lead on the opposite side transfers the image to the surface. Once the paper drawing is removed, I usually redraw the image on with a pencil, as the transfer image is very light and some areas may not have transferred.

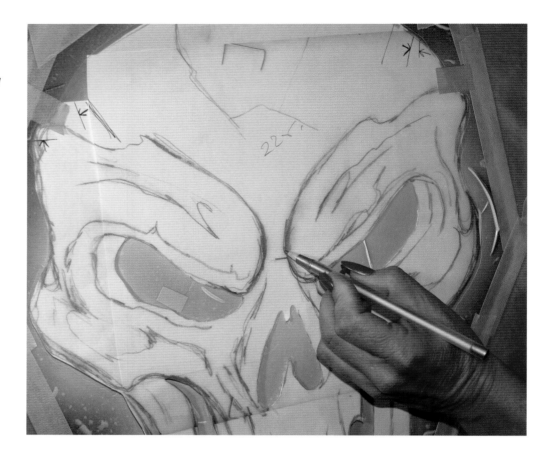

Next, I take those copies I made of the enlarged drawing and cut the detail area out of them for use as stencils—parts like the shadowed areas around the eyes, cheekbones, jaw and such.

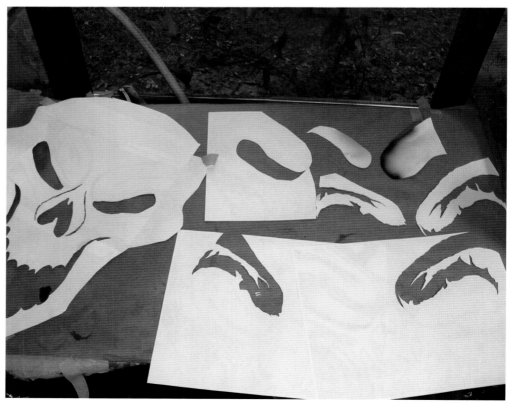

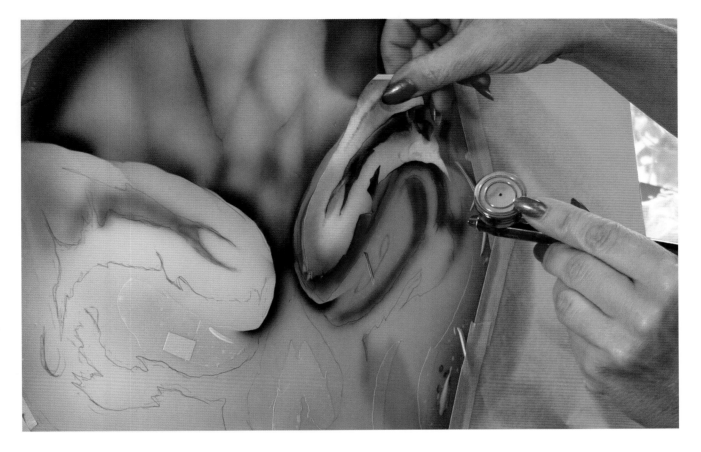

Now mix up the skull colors. I do cool color skulls using white, black, and a blue/black mixture. I mix up the colors thinned down about one part color to two parts reducer, using base coat colors. For the blue/black, I take some reduced black and add some blue base coat toner. I use a very slow reducer, like HOK's RU-312 or PPG's slow reducer. Different paint systems will have different "temps" of reducers. For example, PPG's is DT898, great for very fine detail work. This is where knowing about the paint system you are using comes in handy. I put these color mixes in bottles, then pour out a bit into another bottle and thin it down even more, so you have six bottles with color. Sometimes I will have three different bottles of the same color, only reduced differently: one color to get good coverage, one used for gradual shading, and one to use for very light shading or fine detail work. Use your own judgment to determine what works best for you. I'll be using overreduced color for the dark tones on this skull. I'll start by sketching in the cracked areas, mainly light impressions of cracks and hollows, using the newly cut paper stencils as hand-held shields, using the pencil lines to line up the stencils. I usually start at the top of the skull. I get that area done and proceed to the eyebrows, then eyes. I work my way down. The overreduced blue/black mix is used first, then I softly go over that with the overreduced black. Keep it loose and light. Here you can see where the left brow has already been shaded in with blue/black. Now I do the right side.

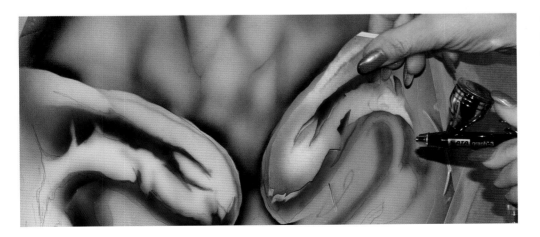

Adding more dark shadows to the brows, I build up the layers of shadows gradually.

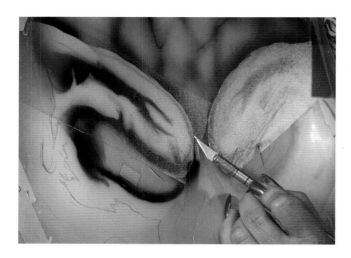

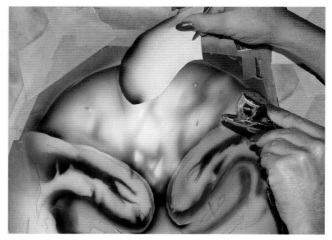

Above left: *The dark colors have been used to rough in the upper part of the skull. Now to start detailing. Strips of TransferRite Ultra Transfer Tape are cut out and laid across the brows, then trimmed with a Number 11 X-Acto knife. I want the area above it to have a clean sharp edge. This will help the brow surface to look as if it were raised above the forehead.* **Above right:** *I load white base coat into the airbrush and lightly brush in the areas between the dark shadows, using the paper stencils anywhere I want a sharp edge to define a crack in the skull. Softly start to build up the high points of the bone surface. Then once the white is on, I go over the dark "cracks" or depressions with both of the darker mixtures, sharpening up the detail. Now I'll do a bit more sharpening up with the white, then pull the airbrush away and apply the white and soften up the whole surface, letting the highlights glow with the white. Now you can see the surface start to take shape.*

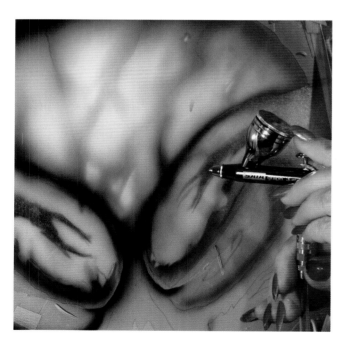

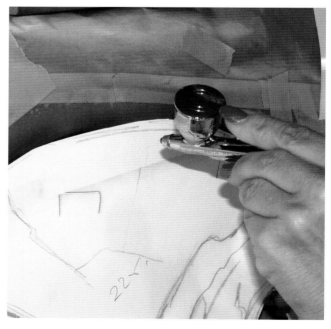

Above left: *I airbrush blue/black along the edges of the brows, then spray up into the "crack" impressions and go over them again very lightly. I repeat this with the black. As these colors are very overreduced, I keep my spray light so it will not run and disturb the paint under it. There are no hard and fast rules here. Just spray a little white and define it with some dark colors. I go back and forth between dark and light, building up the surface impressions of highs and lows. Now, the white tends to make a slight overspray that travels onto the black areas. No matter how low I keep the pressure, it's just something that tends to happen. I usually go back over my black areas (like the eyes) with black and the dark areas (like the eye sockets) with a light wash of the black/blue. It just sharpens up and further defines those areas.* **Above right:** *I want a light edge around the skull, so I hold the original enlarged drawing up the edge of the stencil, leaving a ⅛-inch gap between the drawing and the stencil edge. White base coat is softly sprayed along that gap. As the drawing does not have a smooth edge the whole way around, I have to move it and spray, move it and spray, repeatedly along the edge.*

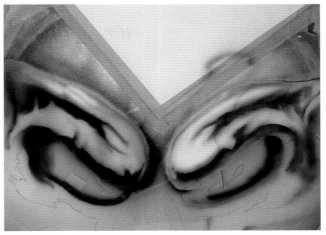

Above left: *Now I'll mask off the forehead using the same technique I used with the brows. And the white detail work begins there, starting with the stencil work. For the eye socket area, use the cut-out copies that were made to lay out the high and low points of the brow and eye socket.* **Above right:** *This photo compares a detailed eyebrow (on the right) to one that is just starting the detail process. The surface of the skull is formed by combined use of freehand techniques and the cutouts.*

HANDY HINT

Note that I have removed the crown caps or spray regulators from my airbrushes. This gives me a finer line.

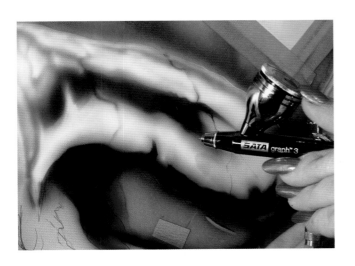

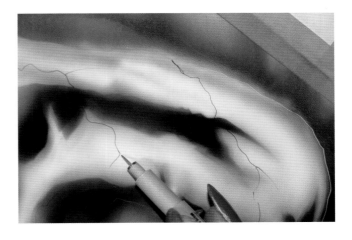

Now I start drawing on the cracks using a fineline marker. In this close-up, the fine detail of all those light layers can be seen.

This picture demonstrates how effective playing around with highlights and shadowing can be. I'm airbrushing the white in the center of the light area, which brings out the high points of the bone surface. The surface comes to life as the white is added. It gives it a 3D effect. Don't expect to get great results in the first five minutes. Getting the results you want will take time. Be patient. It may take a few hours of playing around with your technique before you start to see the bone surface give the illusion of a three-dimensional surface. Little by little, you'll feel more comfortable, and that's when it will start coming together. As for the areas you worked on first that have substandard results? Just go back over them. That's one of the great things about working on murals. You can always go back and rework areas you aren't happy with. Never push yourself the first time you do something new. Give yourself plenty of time and try not to turn it into a torture session. Experiment as you go, play around, find your own technique to get the kind of surface you want.

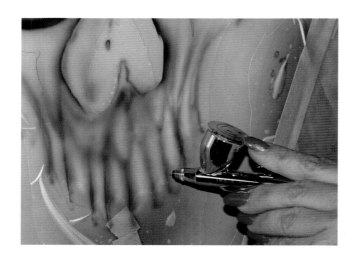

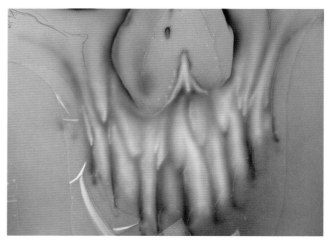

Above left: *The cheek bones and the lower part of the eye sockets will require a lot of stencil use, and I need to let loose and airbrush freehand. So I skip down to the upper jaw area and start airbrushing in the hollows with the dark colors, and then follow that with the white highlights. On the right side the white has been finely airbrushed in, as I work my way over to the left.* Above right: *Compare this picture to the previous one, and note how airbrushing the white in between the dark areas brings form and dimension to the surface.*

HANDY HINTS

Normally, in some cases, I would use magnets to hold the paper stencils in place while I spray them. But this hood is aluminum and magnets won't stick to it. If I really need the stencils to stay in place without holding them and magnets won't work, I'll tape the stencils in place.

Another example of hand-held stencil use. Here the stencil for the dark area under the eye socket is in place. The dark mixtures are airbrushed along its edge.

The stencil is taken away and the newly sprayed shadows can be seen. Note that I have masked off the brows with clear transfer tape. This way, the surface I'm now working on will cleanly end at the brows and appear to go under them.

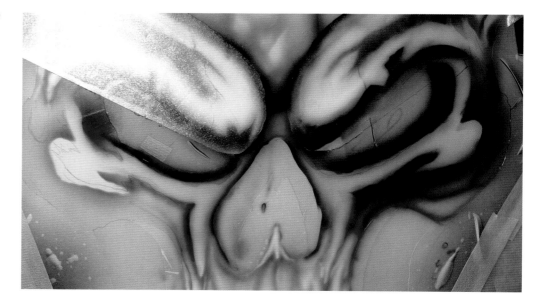

Here the paper stencil for the nose is held up, and the dark tones are airbrushed along the edges.

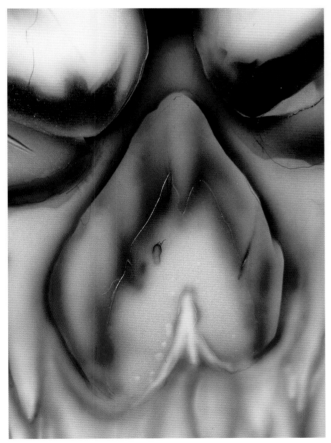

Above left: *The dark tones have been roughed in, and this area is ready for the white tones. Watch how the white really brings this area to life.* **Above right:** *Here I use the leftover frisket paper from when I cut out the mask for the nose opening to create an edge along that opening. It is lined up, leaving a ¹⁄₁₆-inch gap, and white is softly sprayed.*

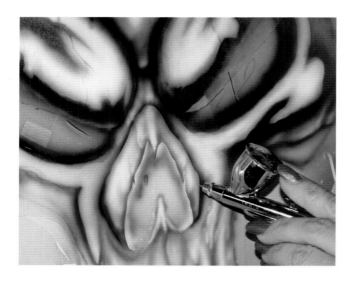
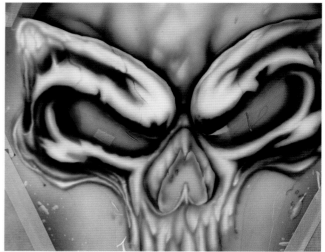

Above left: *Now the white is sprayed in. Note how I've also started spraying the white between the brows. These close-up photos show lots of detail that is not apparent in overall photos.* **Above right:** *Using the same technique of stencils and freehand airbrushing, the cheekbones are finished. The skull is shaping up. I could have added more cracks, and I may go back and add more later.*

Now to paint the jaw! This part of the job will go the quickest. Using clear transfer tape, the upper part of the skull is masked off at the cheekbone. I cut little pieces of transfer tape, and using a Number 11 X-Acto knife, I trim the area on the jawbone away, and then the rest is papered off. I freehand sketch in the depressions in the bone using the blue/black mix and follow that with the black, keeping the shading gradual so the center of the depressions appears to have form. Then white base coat is airbrushed in those areas. The white has only been applied to the right side. I'm working my way over to the left. Some hints for how to "draw" out the grooves in the bone: As you sketch it in with the dark tones, you can sort of see or feel how the texture of bone forms. Note the difference between the left and right sides here. See where I began to add detail with the white and how that gives the bone more form. Once I'm done with the white, I'll go back and airbrush a bit more dark tone in, then just a bit more white.

HANDY HINT

When is artwork done? Completed? Finished? It's hard to say. An artist tends to be his or her own worst critic. There may be things that bug a painter about a certain project. Usually it's something that is a pain in the neck to fix, but something that people will notice. So try and fix those things. But if the artist is going for a certain mood to the artwork, and it just doesn't go in the direction as was hoped for, deadlines will make all difference. There is no easy answer. Each project is different. When I'm faced with a decision like that, I like to talk to another painter to get opinions and then follow my gut. Years ago a painter buddy of mine lost his shop and moved in with me to work until he could find another shop. We kept each other "straight" when it came to realistic expectations. "It's done! Ship it!" was what we told each all the time. Does that mean to skimp on creativity? No, it's very hard to get your best work done when a customer is screaming down your neck. Finish it, move on, and learn from your experiences.

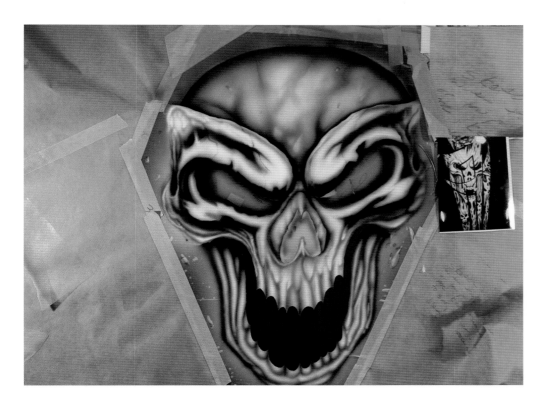

Now the frisket material is removed from the mouth area. See how the exaggerated brows give the skull more attitude. But this guy needs some teeth.

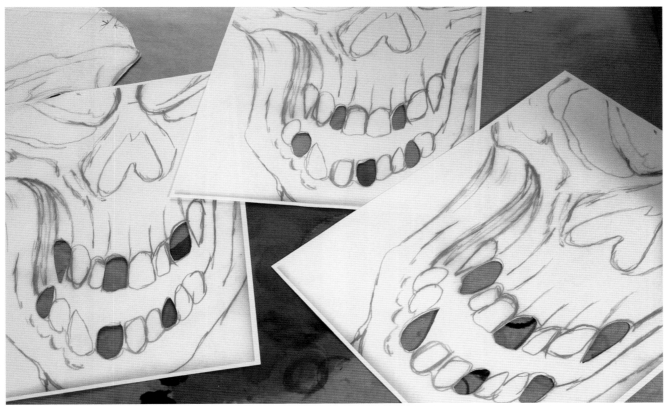

I've made three copies of the lower jaw area of the drawing and cut out a few teeth from each. I leave space between each of the cut-out teeth, or overspray will give me extra ghost teeth.

143

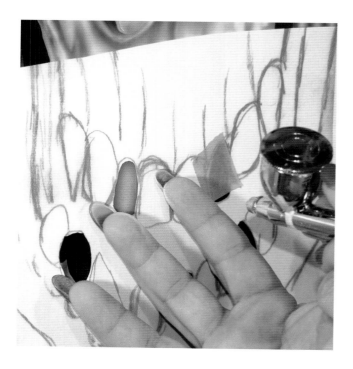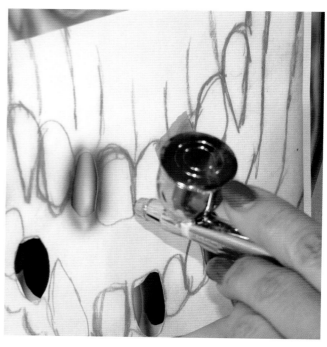

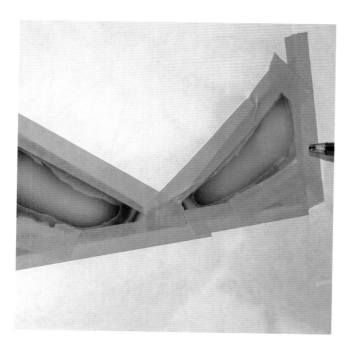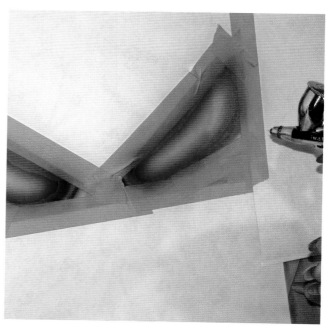

Above left: *As this hood is not steel, I have to tape the paper stencils in place. The thing I have to watch for here is white overspray sneaking under the stencil. So I tape the stencil in place and hold it down with my fingers on each side of the opening. A light coat of white is sprayed.* **Above right:** *Next, both of the dark tones are sprayed on each side of the tooth. Now, you could get creative here and draw cracks on a few of the teeth . . . or play around with shadowing . . . or make the teeth look evil and have them all pointy.*

Above left: *Now the eye holes are masked off with the clear transfer tape and yellow is sprayed. The eyes are another place where you can get some evil effect quite quickly and easily. You could paint actual eyeballs or have real fire coming from them or behind them. Or maybe have skull heads for the irises of the eyeballs. I just want a simple glow.* **Above right:** *House of Kolor Kandy KK01 Brandywine is mixed with some SG-100 and sprayed around the edges. Then a little more yellow is sprayed. Watch out that the colors are not mixed up too thickly as they will spray grainy, and the bottomless effect that is desired here will be lost.*

The skull is unmasked. In most cases, now it would be time for clear coating (see Chapter 14). But this hood is not complete yet. Flames will be going on it. See Chapter 9 for the step-by-step as I add silver leaf flames. Now if this job had been for a customer, I would have done bone effect flames or bone effect webbed graphics radiating out from the skull. But I need an example of leaf work for this book, so Skully here will get some leaf flames. With the right technique, they may just look perfect. Hopefully.

 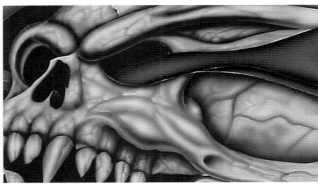

Above left: *The flaming skull on the side of this Corvette is truly evil. The skull was painted first. I had allowed for where the flames would come out of the skull's mouth and eye, as I had the drawing to refer to. That area was masked off and the skull was painted. Then four layers of Spray Mask was brushed on. The flames were cut out and sprayed.* **Above right:** *A close-up of the bone surface detail in previous photo.*

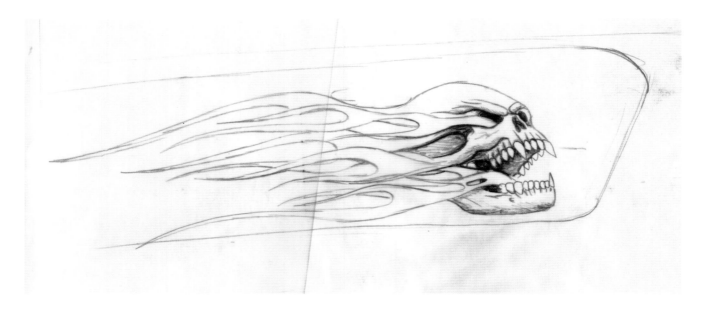

Here is a sample drawing for the flaming Corvette skull.

Please excuse the poor quality of these next photos. This was the customer's idea, to use the taillights as eyes on the back of the same 2002 Corvette.

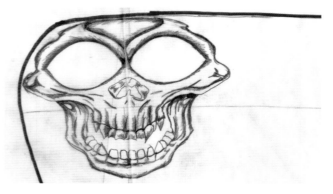

Here is a drawing for the Corvette taillight skulls. I drew up a regular skull and used a computer graphics program to stretch the width.

This is a poor quality photo of a car whose paint didn't turn out too bad.

PAINTING SKULLS

CHAPTER 12
PAINTING A PINUP GIRL

In this chapter, I do a lot more than just paint a cute chick. There's a bunch of great little tricks, like how to paint clouds, how the artwork is designed to fit the surface area, and how to find ideas. I paint more pinups on motorcycles than I do on cars or trucks, but as cars have a much bigger surface area than bikes, they make a great canvas. The images can be painted large, so more detail can be achieved. With enough time and patience, a photorealistic effect can be attained.

So, follow along as I airbrush a sexy witch pinup on the hood of a car. This hood was part of a painting contest for Auto Graphics magazine. I have no idea what vehicle this hood belongs on. I needed a hood and Little Rock Auto Body of Charlotte, North Carolina, let me take a dented part from their junk pile.

The drawing I used for this pinup.

MATERIAL AND EQUIPMENT

White basecoat
Blue tint or toner like HOK KK-04
600-grit sandpaper
TransferRite Ultra Transfer Tape
Pencil
White, brown, black, yellow, red basecoat
Root beer-colored basecoat tint or toner like HOK KK-07
Clear transfer tape
House of Kolor KC-20
House of Kolor UC-35 Kosmic Klear Urethane
Gerson Blend prep tack clothes
EZ-Mix cups
Coast Airbrush's solvent-proof mixing bottles
SATAjet 2000 Digital HVLP gun

Ellipse and circle templates
Low-tack stencil material
#4 Xacto stencil knife
Steel ruler
SATAminijet 4
SATAgraph 3 airbrush
Iwata HP-C airbrush
Iwata Micron C
Light table
Compass
Fineline permanent marker pens such as:
    Pigma Micron 005
    Sakura Microperm 01
    Koh-I-Noor Rapidograph

Here is what I started with. The dents were filled with Evercoat Z-Grip and shaved down with a cheese grater tool before the filler was completely hard. This was followed by an application of 3M Piranna Putty, which was sanded. Then the hood was sprayed with two-part primer/filler. I repeated this process twice and finally the hood was smooth and ready for color.

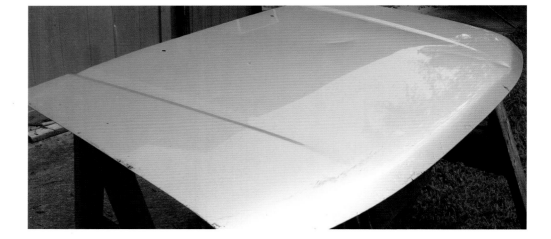

I want the background of the hood mural to be a night sky. I'm trying to obtain a dark gradual fade around the edges so that it is lighter in the center. I start out by mixing white base coat with blue toner, such as House of Kolor BC26 White Base and KK04 Oriental Blue Kandy Koncentrate. This gives me a "lovely" powder blue, a color that doesn't look good on anything, but makes a great undercoat for this project. I apply two coats of this.

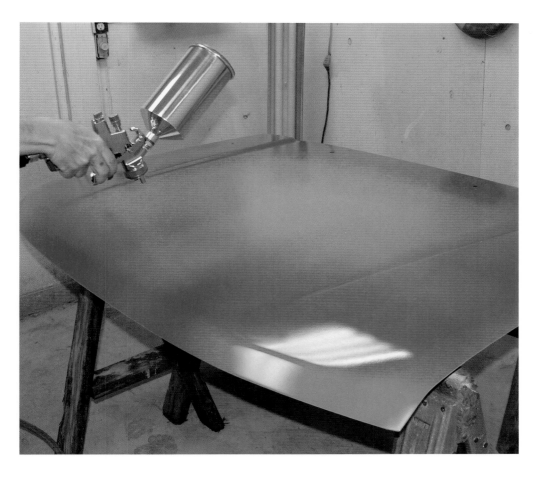

Now I begin the fade around the edge of the hood, using House of Kolor KK04 Oriental Blue mixed with HOK SG-100 Intercoat Clear. The fade is worked toward the center of the hood. Three or four coats are lightly faded in. The trick to getting a clean, nongrainy, gradual fade is to properly mix up the candy paint. I like to use clears with toners or tints in them for my fades rather than premixed candy. This way I can adjust the amount of color. I don't mix much color in candy paint used for fades. If too much color is used, the fade can tend to appear grainy or blotchy. In this case, I mixed just a small spill of blue concentrate into 6 ounces of reduced base coat (SG-100 Intercoat Clear). I use the SATAjet 2000 for the start of the fade, as the HVLP gun very effectively breaks up the paint, giving a nice even spray.

Next I mixed up a mixture of black base coat and blue tint which I reduced down by 150 percent. This was sparely applied around the edges of the hood using a SATAminijet 4. I go around the edge about three times, each time staying closer to the edge. Then two coats of urethane clear are sprayed on. The midnight sky background has a good base. (Note: The reflections on the hood seen in this picture are just reflections from the trees, not part of the artwork.)

I've drawn up the sexy witch seen at the beginning of this chapter. This is where having plenty of reference materials comes in handy. You can use a smile from one photo, eyes from another, and then find the perfect set of legs. Now I need to figure out how big I need the pinup to be. It looks like a pinup of about 21 inches should work. Using the copy function of my printer, I enlarge the drawing 275 percent. Only one section of drawing can be enlarged at a time. So I end up with copies that need to be lined up and then taped together to make one big drawing. I use a light table to see the lines of the drawing through the paper in order to line them up. The surface of the hood is wet sanded with 600-grit. A heavy-duty artist easel works great for mounting the hood. It holds the hood very securely. Whenever possible, it is always better to have the part off the car or truck. I tape the copy to the hood. The size seems right. Now I can see where the clouds need to be and how they will most effectively frame the pinup.

Here you can see the reference photos I used for the clouds. I've collected cloud photos for years, but these are my favorites. First I sketch out the clouds with white base coat. Then I start to build up the cloud surface. The photos help me see where the high spots are. Next a thin mixture of black base coat and blue tint or toner is used.

Torn pieces of paper make great cloud stencils. I use the darks to create low spots. Seeing as how this is a night scene, I'll go over the clouds with a transparent blue toner mixed with base coat clear, like HOK KK04 mixed with SG-100 Intercoat Clear. This mix will be applied over the dark areas and some of the light areas of the clouds. Take care not to apply overreduced paint heavily. Then I'll go over some of the high spots and cloud edges again with white. This way it gives the effect of moonlight hitting the edges of the clouds, having a blue glow over most of them. As you work, you'll either thin down or thicken up the mixtures, and find what works best.

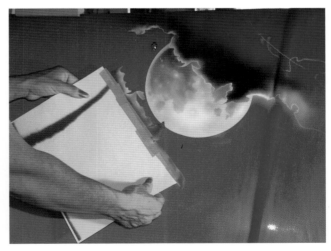

Above left: *What's a midnight ride on Halloween without a full moon? After finding a good reference photo, I enlarge it to the needed size. I place the moon peeking out from under a cloud. After laying a piece of clear transfer tape over the cloud edge to mask it off, I use a Number 4 X-Acto stencil knife to trim off the cloud edge. Using a compass, a pencil line circle is drawn and then taped off with green fineline tape and masked off. I make a paper copy, cut out the darker areas and use that for a moon surface stencil. Notice the dark circles toward the top of the photo? Those are small magnets, which I use to hold nonadhesive stencils or masks in place. I spray a thin mix of black in the dark areas, keeping the shading very random. An ellipse template works great for doing the craters. I'll freehand the white areas, bringing the stroke across the surface of the moon.* **Above right:** *I had not done as much work on the right side of the hood as on the left, and I had only airbrushed a light line where I put the moon. So I had to go back and airbrush the clouds. Clear transfer tape masks off the moon, and the clouds are airbrushed. Then I finish the rest of the clouds.*

151

Using low-tack vinyl stencil mask, like Gerber mask, I lay the enlarged copy of the pinup on a light table, lay the stencil material over it, tape them together and trace the drawing on to the stencil material. You can also use a window if no light table is available. Then the stencil is cut out with a Number 4 X-Acto stencil knife. Press down hard, as you'll be cutting through a layer of mask and a layer of backing. I'll tape thin cardboard on a drawing board and cut against that. This helps in getting a smoother cut. Once the witch is cut out, I'll tape her cutout to the hood surface and arrange her on the hood. I use a 36-inch steel ruler to reference the broom handle. A broom end is drawn on tracing paper and taped into place. Now I can fine-tune how it lays out by moving the pieces around.

The backing is peeled off the stencil pieces and they are placed around the cutout. Now if this were being done on a curved or rounded surface, some of the stencil would need to be cut apart. As it is, a few cuts are made to her. I tape up the cuts with green masking tape. The cutout for the witch will be used as a mask. As the mural progresses, pieces will be trimmed off. Save all those pieces, as they will be used over and over. Curves on the pieces will be used for quick hand-held shields. I line up various curves on the pieces with curves on the artwork. For example, I'll use the curve of a knee as a shield for the curve of an eyelid. And I use these to mask off the areas not being painted at the same time. Here I've cut the boots off and taped them in place. Also, I use them to get nice, sharp edges. First I'll airbrush the legs. Note the main area of the cut-out witch; that part will be put in place over the stencil, and the legs will be ready to airbrush.

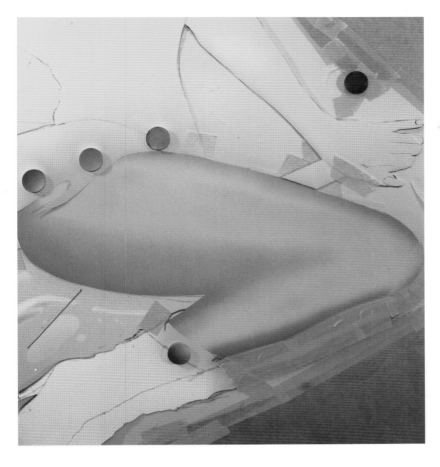

Left: *Here's my mixture for skin tone. Most paint companies have a "root beer"–colored transparent toner or tint. House of Kolor's is KK07 Root Beer. Mix some of this with white base coat, and add just a touch of yellow and red base coat. This can be easily adjusted to be whatever skin tone is needed. Add some white to lighten it up, or add RB (root beer toner) to darken it. I use a reduced version of skin tone (thinned down 150–200 percent) and loosely airbrush in the form of the leg. The lower leg has already been airbrushed and taped off. I use a combination of small round magnets and masking tape to hold the cut-out pieces in place.* **Below left:** *Little by little, I'll gradually build up the shadows. First I'll use a very thinned-down RB toner. If using HOK, mix it with a little SG-100 Intercoat Clear. The lower portion of the leg has been cut out and used as stencil to create a shape shadow, above the calf. Next, a very reduced (150–200 percent) red, is applied right over the RB, maybe extending farther across the surface of the leg, richening up the skin tone. Then, I'll mix some of the RB toner and some black with a medium-brown base coat. This will be the darkest shadow. I keep that localized to the darkest part of the shadow. By the time I'm done mixing colors, I'll have eight colors I'm using: black, root beer/brown/black mix, dark skin tone (darkened w/RB tint), thinned red, regular skin tone, light skin tone, real light skin tone, and white. I have two bottles of each color, one thicker for coloring in, and one thinned down for soft, gradual shading. Exactly how much to thin down is something you'll have to play around with, as each brand of paint is different. Try to keep thinning it down until the paint airbrushes on finely, not grainy. I find the best skin tones are achieved by layering on transparent tones of color. The healthy skin glow is the underpainted skin tones illuminating up through the top layers. Don't airbrush too far along the mask down toward the knee with color, or there will be an unwanted line across leg. Next, I'll remove the lower-leg cutout and airbrush the shadows around the knee and on the lower leg portion. Thinned-down black is used as the last part of the shadowing process. You can see where the shadow goes from black to dark brown to reddish, root beer brown. I'll use my original skin tone to go back and highlight the high spots on the surface of the leg and knee. The cut-out portion of the upper-leg mask will work great as a stencil for the shadow of the ends of the wispy skirt. It is placed just under the skirt and a light coat of black is sprayed.*

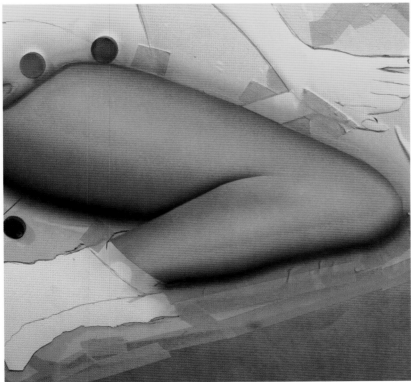

The upper part of the leg mask is used as I airbrush the shadows of the calf. The root beer and red sort of layer over each other. The dark brown is sprayed alongside that, then a touch of black, then the highlights. Use care to not go too far along the mask with the color, or there will be an unwanted line across the knee.

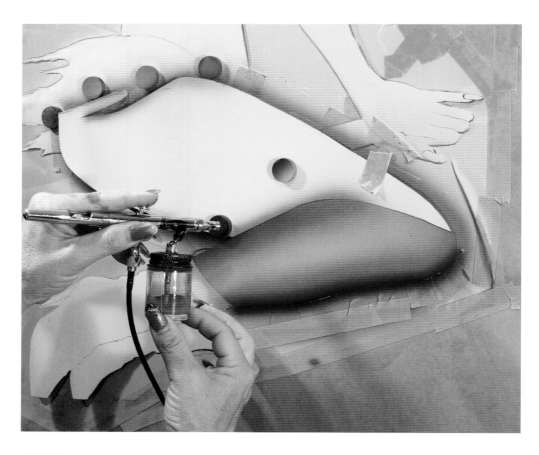

Here is the leg completed. I added a few drops of white to the skin tone color mixture and softly airbrushed highlights. Very lightly, this reduced-down skin tone mixture (200–250 percent) is airbrushed on the high points of the skin surface. These highlights will really bring a rounded form to the body. Basically, this process of masking off different areas, sketching out with skin tone, then adding gradual shading will be repeated throughout the body.

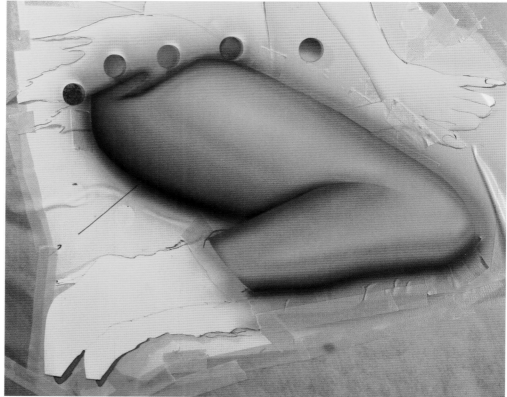

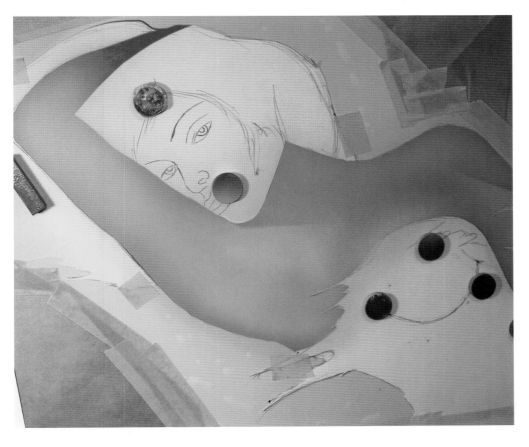

For the upper body, the "clothing" is masked off with the same cutout as is the face. The high points are airbrushed in skin tone. A combination of magnets and masking tape hold the masks in place. The hard edges on the arm and breast are done by airbrushing skin tone against more pieces of the cutout from the original stencil. Then the shadows are worked in using a combination of freehand shading and masks.

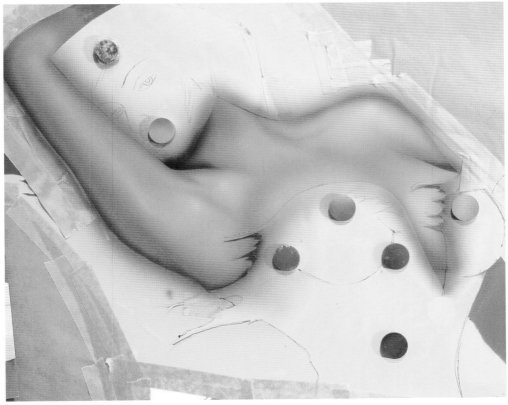

This is where it is great to have reference photos to work from. They can provide a road map of where to airbrush the lights and darks. I keep the "hard" lines of muscle definition to a minimum. You want soft lines, just impressions of shadows where the light goes around a corner of the body's form. Another handy hint is knowing when to stop. At the point seen here I had the optimum effect I was looking for. The only areas that needed more shadowing were the neck and the shoulder to the right. But I kept reworking the shadows in all the upper-body areas.

Here the upper-body piece from the original cutout is used to add a soft black shadow under the fringe of her dress. You can see where the piece of the shoulder was trimmed from the cutout. The dark shadow that defines the breast was created by airbrushing the darker colors along that edge.

Here is the finished result of the upper body. The upper arm disappears into the hair, so I let the paint fade off in that area. I also kept the neck definition to a minimum, as hair will be brought across that area. No sense in doing work that will be covered.

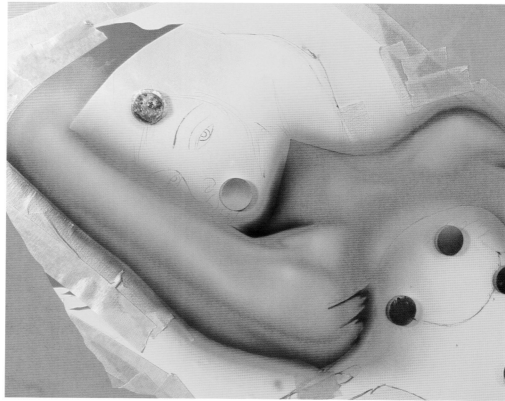

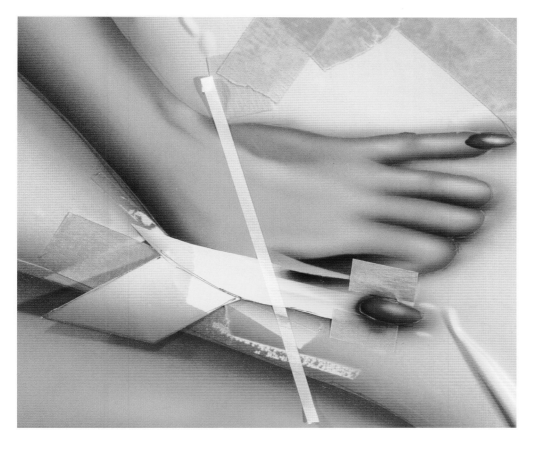

Next the other arm will be airbrushed. Airbrushing the fine detail on hands, wrists, ankles, and feet can be a real pain. Hands may not seem like a big deal, but I find that getting good detail on small items like hands and feet will give an airbrushed body a realistic effect. The hard edges of the fingers are obtained by using various sharp edges on other pieces of the cutout and very soft shadowing. Notice the wrist. There are just a few shadows, but by capturing those effectively, this hand looks like, well, a real hand. The thumbnail is cut from the original yellow cutout and used as a stencil. The detail of the hand is gradually airbrushed freehand.

Now the upper body and legs are masked off. I lay clear transfer tape over the top and bottom of the dress. With a Number 4 X-Acto stencil knife, the dress area is trimmed away. In this photo, the top area and arm have been trimmed. The tape across the bottom needs to be trimmed. I repeat this process to mask off the boots.

Above left: *I won't need to find a photo reference for evil shoes, as I have many pairs of my own to choose from. These "witchy" ankle boots from the 1980s are perfect for my pinup. I pose them at the same angle and position as needed for the drawing and take a picture. I actually did this before I drew the boots for the drawing and used them for reference while I was drawing the boots on the pinup. Now I have a great reference as I am airbrushing the boots, a photo, and the actual boots.* **Above right:** *The dress and boots are airbrushed in black. A very reduced (200 percent) white is used for the highlights. As the pieces from the original cutout are getting more cut up and I want to save them, I use paper copies of the enlarged drawing as stencil masks. Here I've trimmed the fringe from the top of the dress and use the rounded edge for a mask to airbrush the white on the fringe. I also add a fine white edge along the cleavage. As for the folds of the dress, I try to imagine them, and then airbrush them in.*

I do the same thing with the boots, only I use a paper copy of the actual photo I took of the boots. The bottom boot is masked off using tape and a trimmed copy. The heel detail is also obtained by masking off the main boot with a trimmed copy. Using the copies as airbrush shields, with magnets to hold them in place, makes this part of the process go fast.

The face is masked off using a combination of the leftover cutout to mask the hair, tape for the arm, and transfer tape for the jaw line. I'll need to tape a sheet of paper to protect the upper body. This is also the time to make sure that the artwork that has been done is protected from paint that may spill out of the airbrush. I use lids on my airbrush cups, but accidents do happen. Next skin tone is sprayed over the face.

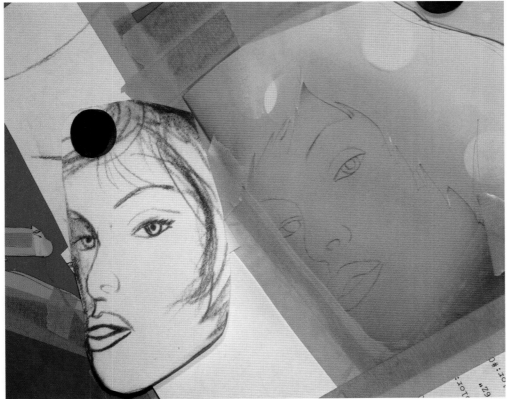

The face is cut out of one of the enlarged copies. It is flipped over and placed on a light table. If a light table is not available, a window will work also. The lines that show through this reverse side are traced in pencil. It is flipped over and lined up over the face. The lines are drawn over with a pencil, and this transfers the drawing to the paint surface. I'll cut out things like the eyes, nose, upper and lower lips, nostril, eyebrows, and other face detail from the other paper copies and use these as stencils to airbrush the face.

Here I'm airbrushing lighter skin tone along the brow and nose, using a paper mask made from a copy. The face still has a long way to go. It's easy to get discouraged at this point, as here she looks anything but pretty. This process is very gradual and takes a while. I use very thinned-down, small amounts of paint. Better to build up the shading slowly, rather than to have to have the colors applied too heavily. Then the face will look spotty. You can always go back and add more.

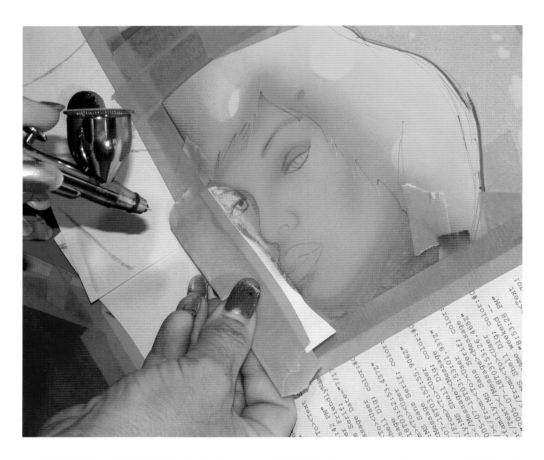

Here you can see where I hold up the nostril stencil and spray just a touch of dark brown. Then I'll spray a little more root beer toner. Take care not to spray too far along the edge when using masks like these, as in this example. I concentrated the spray right at the innermost curve of the nostril to prevent a hard line running up the side of the nose. I'll use separate paper stencils for the upper and lower lips. This process is repeated with a stencil of the nose and right brow area. I just line up the stencils with the pencil lines.

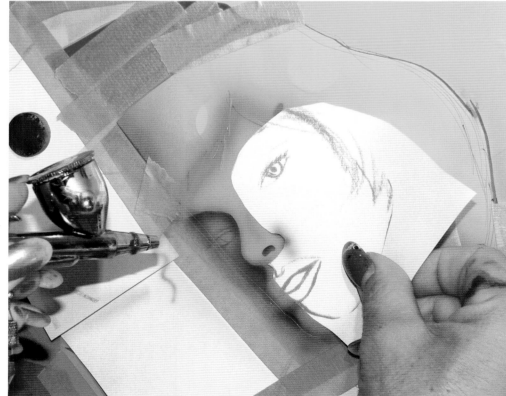

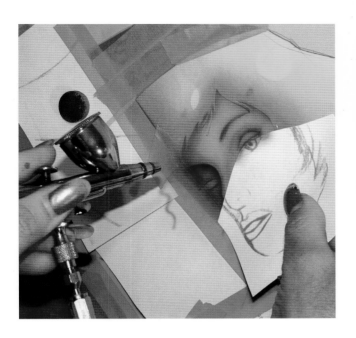 

Above left: *I also look for other shapes that fit various areas, such as the curve of the jaw fitting the outer lines of the eyes. Here I use a paper mask to shade the upper eyelid. I was using a curve from the jaw, but I wanted a very specific shape for the eyes, and it just was not happening. So I switched over the actual paper copy of the eye.* Above right: *A close-up of the progress so far. It's easy to see the soft shading as it is built up. The gentle highlights of light skin tone really bring dimension to the face, just as they did to the body. One thing this photo does not show is how I removed the hair stencil and extended the skin tone past it. I did not like the way the hair framed the face; it wasn't feminine enough. I needed a touch of innocence added to this sexy witch. Seeing more of the face would convey that effect. More forehead maybe.*

Above left: *An eye stencil is cut from a paper copy. The stencil is lined up with the pencil drawing on the face, and white base coat is sprayed. This stencil will be kept in place with tape or magnets, because it is still needed after the white is sprayed.* Above right: *A drafting template with circles is used for the irises. Using the drawing to figure out what size circle will work best, I line up the desired circle and spray brown. See where the stencil for the white part of the eye also masks off the iris? This process is repeated with the pupil. A dot is made in the center of the iris and a smaller circle on the template is lined up over that. Note the small cross lines around the edge of each circle? The intersections of those lines make it easy to line up the center of the pupil.*

Right: *Close-up of the face detail. All the sharp details can clearly be seen. A mix of white and red was used for the lips, and then they were shaded with red, root beer, dark brown, and a touch of black. I went over this face a bunch of times, reworking and fine-tuning it to get this result. I've even drawn on the individual eyelashes using a very sharp black Stabilo pencil. I'm not sure if this will be the final result. What I try to do is get the artwork as close as I can without overworking it. After the artwork is protected with a round of clear urethane, then I'll go back and play around with different things I'm not totally happy with. This way, if my rework is not satisfactory, I can damp sand it off with 600. I'll most likely go over the body with lighter skin tone highlights after the first round of clear. Plus the light line along the jaw will need to be shadowed.* **Below right:** *Next the hair is airbrushed. I don't want to lose any of the hard work I put into the face, so I take the yellow cutout of the face and remove the backing. Along the edge of the hair I cut away about ⅛-inch of backing, then I replace the backing on the back of the yellow cutout. This will protect the face by having the edge along the hair stuck to the surface but not to the area with the face detail. I do not want any adhesive sticking to the detailed area of the face. The arm is masked off with masking tape. First I spray dark brown, and then bring shadows over that with black. Next I use a mix of yellow with a touch of root beer, white, and dark brown. I airbrush lines of that across the hair area. I draw soft lines up to the edge of the face mask. Note how the yellow is away from that edge. I don't want a hard edge of hair around the face. I'll do that area after the stencil is removed. I keep the paint light in the area where the arm disappears into the hair. Next I'll go over it with dark brown and root beer, shadowing areas like where the hair flows from behind the arm. Here you can see where the face area did go beyond the hair stencil. I take care to keep the hair light around those areas.*

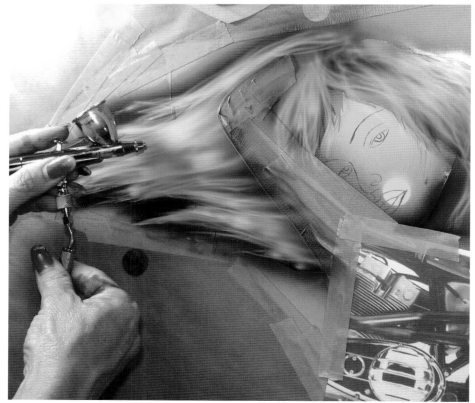

The arm and face stencils (only) are removed and the bits of hair are brought across the arm and neck, and onto the face. First I draw them with the dark brown, and then bring yellow lines over that. The dark brown creates a shadow. Then the whole stencil surrounding the witch is removed.

To remove the stencil, first all the paper and masking tape is carefully removed leaving the original yellow stencil. Note how the stencil is pulled away from itself. This breaks the paint surface as it is removed. Removing the stencil by pulling straight up could result in the paint edge chipping. There may be some bits of adhesive left on the surface from the stencil. These are easily removed with a gentle postsanding precleaner, like HOK's KC-20. Don't rub too hard on the newly painted artwork surface.

Now the broom is taped off with fineline and masking tape. I make sure to tape off the left hand. I lay a piece of clear transfer tape over it and cut out the detail of the hand and fingernail. I cut out the broom end from mask material. The broomstick is laid out with 1/8-inch green fineline tape and masked off the witch's body. Then I paper the rest of the hood to protect it from overspray.

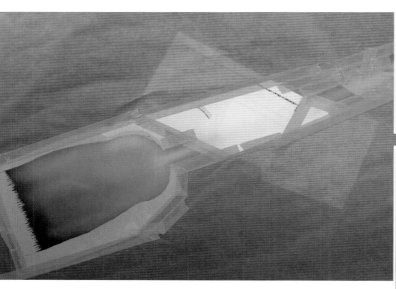

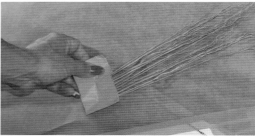

Above: *Then I airbrush loose jagged lines up and down the length of the broom, using the yellow mixture that was used for the hair.* **Inset upper:** *The business end of the broom is masked off. Now I'll make a tool I got the idea for from Jon Kosmoski. I cut actual straws from a broom and lay them across a strip of 2-inch masking tape.* **Inset lower:** *Then dark brown and black are sprayed through the broom straws. Next the root beer toner is airbrushed in various places. Then a few lines of the yellow to highlight. The browns are then used to shadow the broom handle. A few passes with this and the broom is done. Now all masking material is removed from the hood. Four or five coats of clear urethane, such as HOK UC-35 Kosmic Klear Urethane, go on next. The first layer is sprayed on lightly, so it doesn't grab hold of the artwork, soften it up, and blur it. I let it dry overnight.*

Here's the witch so far. You can see how the fading, the frame effect of the clouds, and light source of the moon all come together. I think I'll add some fire coming out from the broom. It needs something more to balance it out, like bringing some yellow into the bottom half of the hood. There are a few other things I want to do, but the clock is ticking, and other projects are waiting to be worked on. I have to wrap this up. The hood is wet sanded with 600 and brought into the studio.

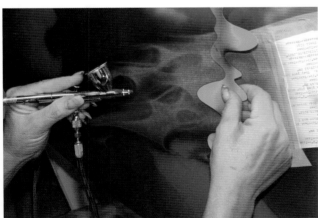

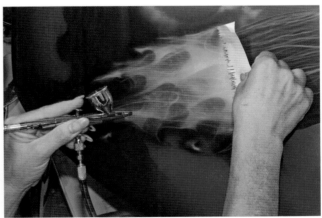

Above left: *I'll use the cutout leftover from the broom stencil to mask off the end of the broom. Real fire effect is airbrushed on. First the flames are loosely drawn on with House of Kolor SG103 Molly Orange. The curves are defined using Artool Freehand Shields. Next a candy red is sprayed on. I use HOK KK11 Apple Red mixed with SG-100 Intercoat Clear. The process is repeated, but instead of applying candy red over the flames, I used candy orange (HOK KK08 Tangerine). Refer to Chapter 7 for more info.* **Above right:** *The process is repeated again, but this time yellow flames (HOK SG102 Chrome Yellow) is used to draw on the flames. The flames are sharper and tighter. And fewer of them are applied. Candy orange is applied in areas that need to be shadowed. Then HOK KK12 Pagan Gold is mixed with Intercoat Clear and applied over all the flames. A few more yellow highlights are airbrushed on. All the masking materials are removed. I use the backing leftover from the end of the broom as a hand-held shield and spray more yellow on the very beginning of the fire. Any overspray from the fire is wet sanded off. I then decide there is too much fire. So all the fire is wet sanded off, and I completely redo the fire, but this time there is less fire, and it is sleeker. I airbrush more strands of hair where it flows across the sky. Now the car goes back into the booth, where I spray on three coats of House of Kolor UC-01 Kosmic Urethane Klear using a SATAjet 2000 HVLP spray gun. I love this gun.*

And here she is on her midnight ride. You can see the redone fire. Unfortunately, during the clear coat process a small bug landed in the wet clear. In trying to dig it out, I went through the yellow of the hair. This will need to be touched up before the final clear coat.

Super close-up of the face. I think I may add a few more eyelashes. I'll draw them using either a black Stabilo pencil or a very fineline permanent marker such as Pigma's Micron 005, Sakura's Microperm 01, or Koh-I-Noor's Rapidograph. Then I'll softly airbrush some black over the added lashes. I always seem to find other changes I would like to make.

Close-up of the redone fire.
Reflections make it hard to take
good pictures.

I see the skin tone is lighter on the face than on the body, so the body will need to be lightened up slightly. This is why it's a
good idea to have clear protecting the artwork when fine-tuning. If you don't like the rework, it can simply be wet sanded
away without damaging the original artwork. But for now this witch is done.

A FEW OTHER MURALS

Above left: *Here's the front view of the Corvette seen at the end of Chapter 11. Flames, lightning, and an eagle.* **Above right:** *Here is the drawing for the Vette hood art.*

PAINTING A PINUP GIRL

Above left: *Here is a very pretty lady on the hood of a Cadillac. But this hood is not mounted on a car. Instead it is part of a trailer owned by orthodontist Dr. George Pinsak of Charlotte, North Carolina. He specializes in braces and wanted to inspire his patients. The photo was taken at an odd angle as the hood was down.* **Above right:** *Of course, I had to take a picture before her braces went on. But unlike Dr. Pinsak's patients, her braces will remain forever. I did this paint in 1998.*

CHAPTER 13
SERIOUS FUN WITH PINSTRIPING

Ah, pinstriping. I leave that to the experts, guys like Ryan here. He wanted to help me out with a pinstriping chapter for this book. It would take a whole book to thoroughly cover this incredible art, so this is a crash course in this time-honored craft. There are two kinds of pinstriping: graphic pinstriping and traditional hot rod striping.

Ryan Young of Indocil Designs is one evil pinstriper. He takes his craft very seriously. Ryan no longer does pinstriping on vehicles. These days he only does helmets, for which he is quite famous. But he made an exception for my little truck graphic project.

EQUIPMENT

Striping brushes come in two types, natural and synthetics. While natural brushes hold more paint, due to the microscopic scales along the shaft of the hair, synthetics are said to be more durable, easier to clean, and recommended to be used with acrylic paints. But most artists use natural brushes, most of which are made of squirrel hair. Most stripers use a "00" or a "000," depending on the desired width of the stripe. Ryan uses Mack Sword Striping brushes. Check out www.mackbrush.com and look over their extensive line of brushes. Their website is a library of information about striping brushes. Every striper will find the brush that works best for them.

The two main kinds of brushes are swords and daggers. Swords have their longest hairs on the top and taper back to a short length on the underside. Daggers are double-edged, come to a point, and work well for small, curved work. Most artists use the swords. Brushes range in cost from about $6 to $25.

Each company has its own system of numbers for brush size. The bigger the number, the more paint it holds. For example, a Mack "00" is bigger than a "000." Most stripers trim and reshape their brushes. But too much trimming can take away the softness of the brush. Ryan likes to trim his brush right down to the tip, taking about 1/32 inch off the tip, giving it a blunt shape, rather than keeping the sharp

MATERIAL AND EQUIPMENT

Mack "000" Sword Striper

Can bottoms for holding solvents

Palette knife for mixing paint in cans and opening the cans

House of Kolor Urethane Striping and Lettering Enamel

House of Kolor U-00 Reducer

Lacquer thinner

Mineral oil

Disposable gloves

Small paper cups

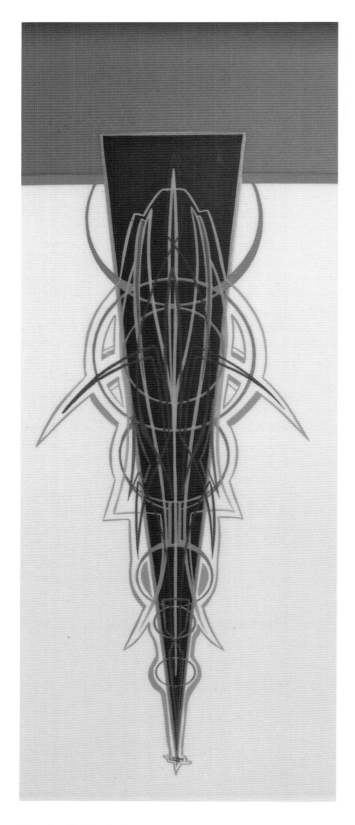
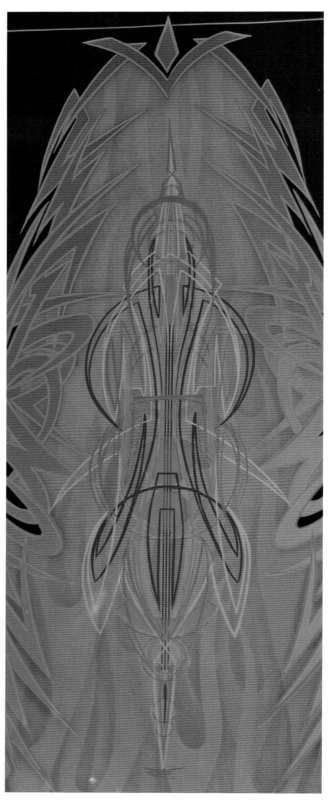

Examples of traditional pinstriping. Traditional striping is something that takes years and countless hours of trial and error to perfect. Each striper develops his or her own distinct style.

point. A new brush always needs to be cleaned before it is used. Hold it under a stream of water and wash it out with dish soap. Then dry and oil it. To trim it, wet down the hair, lay it flat on a palette, and use a razor blade to cut straight down. Take care not to trim too much from the belly or midsection of the brush or change the way the paint flows through the brush, or the brush will leave dry stripes from too much hair at the tip. So go easy on the trimming.

STRIPING BASICS

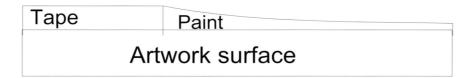

Always stripe over clear and sanded artwork. Don't stripe over uncleared paint edges. The reason is that paint levels are never level. This illustration shows how paint will settle into taped-off artwork areas, forming ridges next to the taped off border. The sharp ridge will stick through the painted stripe because the stripe paint will settle around the ridge. The pinstripe will look like a hairline crack is running through it. So protect your artwork with urethane clear and wet sand that ridge down. Have a nice, fresh surface to work on. This also allows for mistakes. If you screw up, simply wet sand it away. Wet sand the surfaces to be striped with 600 and wipe dry.

Ryan is using House of Kolor Urethane Striping Enamel. Urethane-based paints are great for striping, as they can be easily clear coated over. You'll also need two tins to hold solvents. Coffee cans, cat food cans, or the bottoms of soda cans can be used. Fill one with lacquer thinner for cleaning brushes, the other with reducer. Ryan is also using House of Kolor Urethane Striping Enamel Reducer. There are two ways to palette, or load, a brush. The first way uses a phone book, glossy magazine, or catalog. Those free real-estate magazines are popular. Dip the brush in the reducer, then in the paint, and brush it back and forth on the magazine surface. This is referred to as paletting. You're looking for a certain amount of drag. If it is too dry, dip it in the reducer and repalette. You want consistency, paint not dripping off the brush but pulling easily out of the brush, leaving a smooth line.

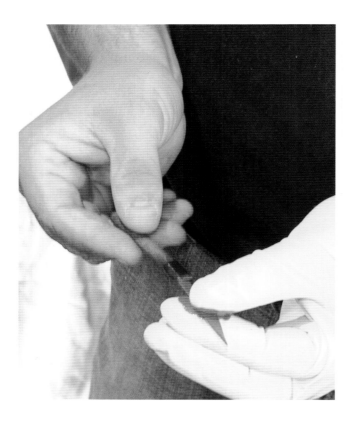
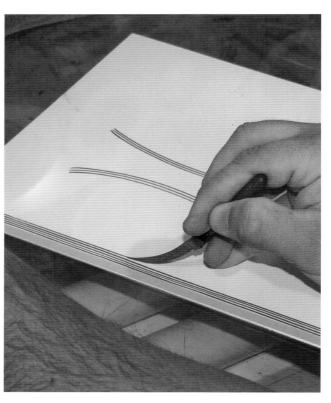

Above left: *The second method of paletting, and the one Ryan uses, is to use his finger to load the brush. Dip the brush in the paint, then in the reducer and pull the brush through your forefinger and thumb until you feel the paint consistency you want. Ryan likes the added control to form the bristles, as it is being paletted. Once the brush is loaded, start striping.* Above right: *Practice lines on sign blanks or test panels. It is the only way to learn the proper paint consistency and line quality. Lay down a piece of tape, and then use it as a guide for your stripe. Set the brush down about 1/32-inch from the tape without touching it. Place your pinky on the edge of the tape. You want your hand to be in a locked position or motion, using your finger as a guide. Before striping your first part, practice, practice, practice!*

Here Ryan is striping a free-floating line on a helmet. There is no graphic or flame line to use as a reference. A ¼-inch strip of masking tape is run around the helmet just below where the stripe will be. Leave about a ¹⁄₃₂-inch gap above the tape. Don't touch the tape with the brush. It is only used a gauge. Start your stripe, keeping the pressure steady and smooth, pulling the brush across the helmet. Note how Ryan has the helmet on its side so it's in a comfortable position for him to stripe. Always try to find a striping position where you're at ease, so you can relax and concentrate on pulling a clean line.

HANDY HINT

No striper can pinstripe well without quality music. You have to get into the groove and get your head in the right place. Relax and enjoy the striping experience.

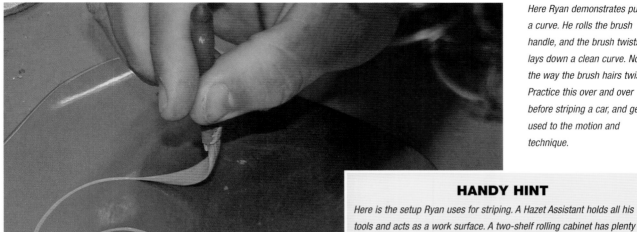

Here Ryan demonstrates pulling a curve. He rolls the brush handle, and the brush twists and lays down a clean curve. Note the way the brush hairs twist. Practice this over and over before striping a car, and get used to the motion and technique.

HANDY HINT

Here is the setup Ryan uses for striping. A Hazet Assistant holds all his tools and acts as a work surface. A two-shelf rolling cabinet has plenty of space for many cans of paint, and it also provides more work surface.

STRIPING GRAPHICS

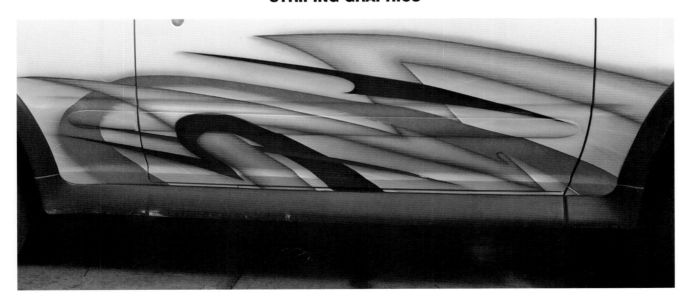

Here's my truck after I painted the graphics. It looks good, but striping will really bring those layers to life.

The yellow/orange graphic will be striped first. I want a yellow stripe on it, but it needs to show up against the yellow. So Ryan mixes a custom yellow from three different stock yellows.

The yellow stripe shows up great against the yellow/orange graphic. Unlike a helmet or a motorcycle part, you can't adjust a vehicle to get a comfortable striping position. So the striper must position his or her body so they can relax and concentrate on the stripe. Cardboard is laid on the ground and Ryan stretches out on it to stripe this bottom area of the truck.

A custom lime green is mixed up to stripe the blue area. Note how Ryan is using his pinky against the surface of the truck to steady his hand and act as a guide. His other hand also helps to keep his striping hand steady.

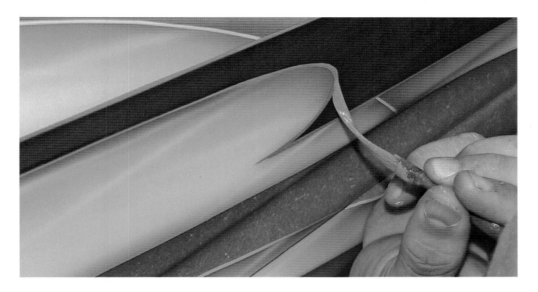

A custom purple mix is used for the dark-purple stripe. Notice the way the brush twists as the handle of the brush is rolled as it goes around the curve.

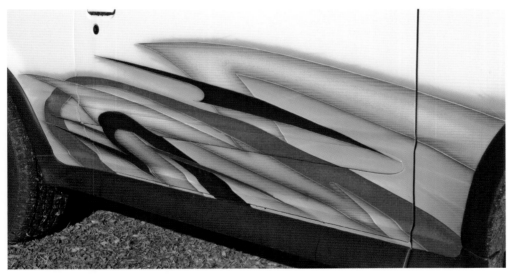

The finished result. What a difference the striping makes. Wow! I love my truck. I may actually have to keep it clean now.

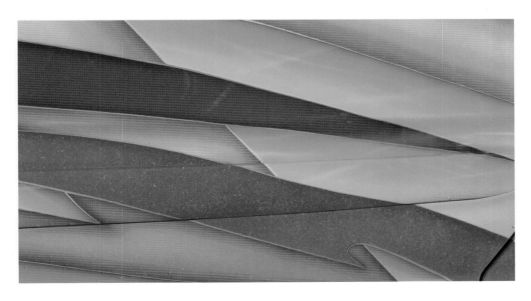

OK, you've striped something and it's awful. This is the perfect opportunity for slash striping. In fact, maybe that's how it got started. But this is when you critique your striping and make adjustments. Always make an honest effort to pinstripe a project before you resort to slash striping. One day it will be good enough and you'll be proud. All those hours of practice will have paid off.

SLASH STRIPING

Many inexperienced stripers start out by slash striping. But they are only cheating themselves out of valuable striping experience. First, stripe the graphic or flame with a regular stripe, no matter how bad it looks. Then begin the slashes. The reason? You'll gain hours of valuable striping experience and be able to cover up any flaws with the slashes. This is a test panel for a truck paint job.

Slash right over the top of the pinstripe you laid down. Just crisscross over it in a random fashion. This will hide any flaws.

FINAL FINISHING AND CLEAN-UP

Never apply heavy coats of clear over your striping. The weight of the clear can literally drag down the stripe. Refer to Chapter 14 for more information.

House of Kolor recommends that you do the final wipe down with their KC-20 or water only. Solvent-based precleaning wash products will remove the artwork. Mistakes over catalyzed urethane are easily removed with a rag dampened with acetone.

Cleaning the brush is very important. Rinse the brush in the lacquer thinner until no paint comes out. Then dip it in mineral oil. The oil keeps any remnants of the paint from drying up and helps the bristles retain their natural oils.

A FEW MORE EXAMPLE OF STRIPING

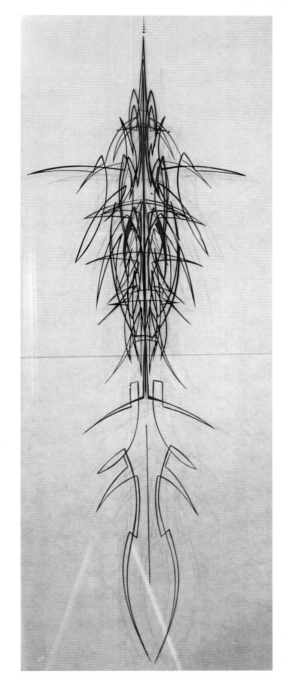

Above: *Another example of slash striping.* **Below:** *This sweet, one-color design is located at the very front of a hood. A small but very effective detail.* **Left:** *I love the way this striped creation is done on glass. The design is strong and clean.*

CHAPTER 14
CLEAR COATING, THE LAST PAINT STEP

Nothing feels better at the end of a long paint project than to reach the point of spraying clear coat. Then again, there is no worse painting hell than spraying that clear coat and watching serious paint problems happen right before your disbelieving eyes. It's a heart-stopping moment every painter has lived through. So the clear coat application is not the time to sit back and relax. Pay careful attention to what could be the last step of your custom paint job, or it will be your introduction to painting hell.

There are two ways painters clear coat their base coats: Some painters will use base coat clears (sometimes with hardener added) for everything but finish clear, as base coat clear is not designed for use as a final clear top coat. Other painters will use urethane clear and only urethane clear for nearly everything. This is a question that you'll only answer with experience. Shop conditions, equipment, personal preferences, and weather can determine what works best for any particular painter.

Base coat clears can be the way to go. They're less expensive than urethane clear, and in some cases they dry harder and faster, especially if hardener is added. If a painter is on a tight budget, base coat clear is something to be considered.

Use whatever clear coat method you are comfortable with. I use urethane for my candy mixes because I like the

This is some glassy clear. It's almost like looking into a mirror. You can see very pebble on the ground, the clouds in the sky, even the photographer.

way it hardens up so fast. I'm used to using it and it works very effectively for me. I do my filler clear with urethane clear for the same reasons. Plus, I do a lot of rework using frisket film, and it tends to leave adhesive residue on anything other than urethane. I also like using a clear that dries rock hard overnight, but not too hard to accept recoating. If the clear is too hard, like some of the totally rock-hard uro clears, there may be problems with delamination. I need a clear I can cut frisket on, something that is very forgiving when it comes to how long you can wait to spray in between coats—the window. Some clears have a very tight window, others are more lenient, and I need all the help I can get. I use products that cut me slack.

Urethane clear is heavy. And if not applied carefully, the weight of the uro clear and its flow-out will cause it to run very easily. It can literally drag down any artwork that was applied, smearing and running it. Most of the surfaces on a car are vertical, so this can really be a problem. I use a fast urethane clear like House of Kolor UC-35.

Many brands of urethane clears have several kinds of hardener that can be used. A slower hardener is best used for finishing clear coats, which won't need as many coats as a filler clear. Superfast hardeners dry quicker but tend to not flow out and give that glasslike finish desired in a final clear. The slower hardener may take a few days to thoroughly dry, but it will flow out beautifully and retain that wet look. It makes them more of a challenge to paint, as the slower-drying paint has time to form sags and runs. Have a plan of attack, know where the coats will start, and know the path the spray gun will take as it moves over the car.

MATTE FINISH CLEARS

While glassy finish clear coats are the most common, many painters are now opting for satin or matte finish clear coats. I see more and more "rough" hot rods cleared with a flat finish. It gives evil attitude to cutting-edge projects. These are finishes that have varying degrees of gloss, and in some cases there is no gloss at all. Satin finish clear coats have a slight sheen to them, like satin. Matte finish clear coats have no gloss at all. The crazy part is that the same urethane clear is used for both glossy clear coat and nonglossy clear coats. The difference is that a flattening agent is used. Most paint companies have product like House of Kolor's FA-01 Flattening Agent.

The amount of gloss that will show depends on how much flattening agent is mixed in with the clear. For example, if you're using HOK's FA-01, 2 ounces of flattening agent added to a quart of ready-to-spray urethane clear will result in a 10 percent gloss reduction. Four ounces added will result in a 25 percent gloss reduction. (Six ounces

HANDY HINT

One of the big drawbacks to using urethane clear is how heavy it is and how well it flows out. This can result in extra material accumulating around the edges of the fenders, particularly the ends. Keep a lookout for this each time you sand a filler coat of urethane clear. Take care to only sand the run, not the area around it. You don't want to sand through your color coat. I use 600-grit paper wrapped around a hard sanding block like Motor Guard's Run Blocker and/or the edge of my finger. This is one of the reasons some painters prefer using base coat clear with hardener, as it does not tend to pile up on edges.

equals 60 percent, 8 ounces equals 90 percent, 12 ounces equals 95 percent, 16 ounces equals 99 percent.) The best way to go is to try out your mix on a test panel and know the exact amount of flattening agent needed for the amount of gloss reduction that is desired.

In most cases, additional reducer will need to be added for proper sprayability. The amount of reducer to be added depends on how much flattening agent as used. For example, if using 4 ounces of FA-01 in your clear, add 1 ounce of extra reducer.

Strain the clear into your gun and apply as you would any urethane clear. Gloss reduction will begin as the paint dries. Drying overnight will reveal just how much gloss reduction there is.

IF CLEAR COATING OVER ARTWORK

I usually wet sand carefully around any artwork after I finish the artwork and have removed the tape or stencil material. I use 600 or 800 paper and only lightly sand the area that did not receive any artwork, carefully sanding around the artwork. It removes any foreign objects, like overspray or drips that have found their way onto the surface.

Never touch the parts with your hands. I keep a clean, wet washcloth in the hand I hold the vehicle with, keeping that against the surface. There are a couple reasons for this: It keeps contaminants from my hand off the painted surface, and it helps keep water on the part as I wet sand.

After wet sanding, I wipe the part down very thoroughly with the wet washcloth and then rinse the part off. Let the vehicle air-dry, but after the parts have dried a bit use a paper towel and wipe away any remaining water drops and any water that has accumulated on the fender edges. The main reason for removing this water is so that minerals won't remain on the parts after the water has dried up. This

Check out the roof of Britt Spring's 1955 Chevy. A flawless clearcoat will add depth to any paint job.

can be a real problem if your shop is in an area with hard water or you use well water. You can use compressed air to blow off the water immediately after wet sanding, but make sure your air source is very clean and well filtered. No sense in blowing dirty, oily air onto a fresh, clean surface.

If you use urethane clear over artwork, the first two coats should be sprayed lightly and allowed to set up; then heavier coats may be layered on. I learned all of this the hard way, having to go back and rework my artwork after heavy coats of uro clear took the uncleared base coat paint I used in my artwork and ran it right down the side of a truck. But the first coats must not be sprayed on too heavy. They have to be very light, but they must provide decent coverage that "locks down" the artwork. After spraying the lock-down coats, I do a medium coat, and then follow with several heavy hammer coats—heavy enough to flood plenty of clear over the paint edges, but not heavy enough to form runs or sags.

The next day, or when it is hard enough, I wet sand with 600, wrapping it around a medium soft block like Meguair's Hi-Tech Sanding Backing Pad. Again, don't let accumulated water dry on the top surfaces of the car and don't touch the surface with bare hands. I use paper towels in my hand to hold against the parts. I never touch a ready-to-clear surface without a paper towel between the surface and my hand. I do this because fingerprints will show through as visible imperfections in the finished clear-coated paint. It doesn't happen often, but once is too many times. So I take care with every vehicle I paint.

Another area painters disagree on is wet sanding grits. Six hundred grit or less? The trick is to have a good enough tooth for the clear to bite into, but not have to worry about sand scratches appearing in the clear coat surface as it dries. Jon Kosmoski recommends using 600 for wet sanding, as anything with less grit could lead to delamination problems.

The main areas plagued with delamination problems are places where parts are bolted against painted surfaces, like mounting areas for door handles, mirrors, and other trim pieces. A bolt gets tightened down against the painted surface, twisting against it, and trying to grab it; it pulls up the paint, tearing it away from the metal. Usually the primer and base coat stick, and only the urethane paint color (candy and clear) separate. These parts were not designed to have 20 coats of paint on them. So the heavily coated surface gets squished against the mounting, and the many soft coats of urethane puddle up. I try to somehow apply as little paint on these areas as possible. For example, if I am clearing over artwork, trying to smooth out some paint edges, I'll flood the clear only over the artwork, staying away from any mounting holes. And I make sure I very thoroughly sand any mounting area each time I sand, starting with the primer. But watch out that you don't sand through on the sharp corners.

Edges of hoods, fenders, and trunk lids can also be problem areas if they did not receive enough prepaint preparation. Many times, these areas get poor prep, as the painter will sand down the flat side of the panels and not bother to slide the sandpaper in between the breaks between them. Always open hoods, doors, and trunk lids and sand those edges.

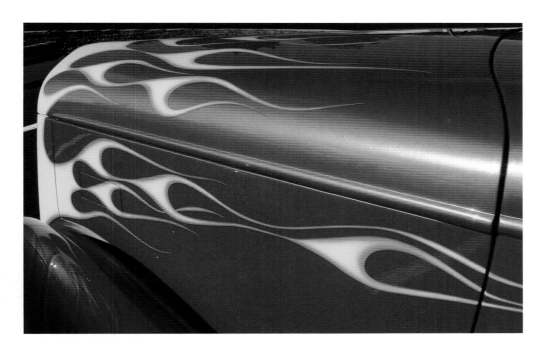

Finish clear coat is the last step to a great paint job. It doesn't matter how much work was put into any particular job if the finish clear is anything less than perfect.

FINISH CLEAR COATS

Deadlines and complaining customers don't always allow the time for paint to dry properly. It would be nice to spray a few coats of finish urethane clear, wait a week, wet sand it with 600 or 800, and spray another round of coats. But more often than not, painters get to spray a clear coat round one day and follow it the next day with the second and final round.

As for me, I don't recommend baking custom paint. I find that paint edges, especially on graphics and flames, are more pronounced on baked paint. I'm sure other painters could speculate and argue with me why that happens, but the point is it has happened to me so I don't bake finish clear coats.

There is a myth about the best amount of clear coat to have on a paint job. Some say the more clear coats, the better. This is not true. While it's necessary to have enough clear coat to give depth to single-color paint jobs and level out mutilayered paint work, 5 coats of clear will survive longer down the road than 20 coats of clear. The reason for this is the sharp edge around every panel. The more paint applied, the more paint piled up around that sharp edge of the hood, fenders, etc, and the more chance there is of chipping. A thicker paint surface will extend that edge beyond the end of the panel. It won't extend by much, but even 1/16 inch of paint thickness will be prone to chipping easier than 1/32 inch as there is no metal directly under it to give it strength. Unless the vehicle is used strictly for car shows, normal wear and tear will happen. And no matter how hard a person tries to take good care, chips happen,

and the custom painter will find the customer back at the shop a year later requesting that these little chips be fixed. And in the case of candy paint, this can be not a quick fix.

The number of clear coats you should apply will vary with each paint job. A single color will require maybe only 2 to 3 coats of clear urethane. A paint job with multiple layers of artwork will require maybe 15 coats of clear. Keeping the clear layers to a minimum where the parts will bolt against other parts will help greatly in keeping the paint job looking good over time. This is an area where common sense and experience will help a painter determine what works best.

One last thing to remember about finish clear coats is that they flow out over time. This means that while the clear may not look completely flat and glassy at first, a few minutes later it will flow out to the perfectly smooth surface you desire. This is why a painter needs to be very familiar with the product being used. Clear coat paint materials are usually the costliest part of any project, so don't waste them. And don't waste time by having to do rework. If you're unfamiliar with a product being used, test it on a spare panel before using it on a whole car. Know how heavily it can be applied before it runs or sags. Know how long it will take to flow out. Know how long it will take to harden. Remove all the "unknowns" from any paint situation . . . well, as many as you can.

BUFFING

I try to be a good person, because my idea of hell is spending eternity subjected to something that you absolutely hate. And I hate buffing. Even though there are many handy dandy tools that make buffing not so unpleasant, I still hate to buff. Maybe there have been too many traumatic buffing experiences in my past. Too many times I was finished, and I mean done, with a job. Then I saw one little bit of dust that didn't quite buff all the way flat. I sanded it down just a bit with 2,000-grit, hit it ever so slightly with the buffer, and watched in horror as a spot opened up, indicating that I had gone through a round of clear coat. I honestly didn't think I would survive, standing there, buffer in hand, waiting for my heart to stop. After my blood started flowing again, I'd get out the 800 sandpaper, wet sand the part, and head back into the booth for another round of clear.

I can't go back there. So I leave buffing duties to others . . . actually, a sturdy young man with a strong heart. He's younger than me, not by much, but he has the disposition for buffing.

Me? I know the devil is waiting for me. He's got a buffer with a nasty pad, cheap polish, and an endless mountain of car and motorcycle parts. I have no choice but to be good.

There are many companies making products specifically designed for final sanding clearcoat. Hutchins' Water Bug III Sander uses the 3M Hookit sandpaper system with a hose dipped into a water bucket. It provides a steady source of water as you do your final sand. It makes short work of sanding cars. Other painters simply use a palm DA sander with 1,500-grit paper and a spray bottle of water.

But here's the recipe for buffing from the Clear Coat Master Himself, Wayne Springs of Little Rock Auto in Charlotte, North Carolina:

"Wet sand bits of dust and other boogers with 2,000-grit. Dry the part, and make sure all the "bugs" are out. Next I use Hi Gloss Clean Cut Non-Silicone Auto Compound (Number 32101 made by EZ-1, Stockton, CA, 209-948-1133).

"Buff out with the Clean Cut to a high gloss using 3M Perfect-It foam pad Number 05723. Then rinse any Clean Cut off the car. Then go over the car with 3M Perfect-It Foam Pad Polishing Glaze Number 05996 using a 3M Perfect-It foam pad Number 05725. Then wipe the car down with Meguiar's Number 7 Glaze."

CARE AND UPKEEP OF YOUR CUSTOM PAINT

Easy quiz: What causes most scratch damage to paint jobs?

A. Rocks and gravel on rough roads.

B. Lame idiots touching the painted surface with rings on.

C. Dogs, cats, or other animals jumping on the vehicle.

D. Washing.

Answer: It's D! Most of the surface scratches any painted surface will receive will happen during washing. Tiny rocks, specs of sand, and particles of dirt get trapped in sponges and washing materials, and it's almost like sanding your car while you wash. So here is how I wash any custom painted surface.

First, fill a clean bucket with water and a wax-free soap. (I mean a clean bucket. Rinse it out real well. In fact, you should dedicate a bucket for washing only.) Then go into the house and get a clean washcloth from the linen closet. Using a good sprayer on the end of the garden hose, rinse the vehicle from top to bottom, removing as much debris as possible.

Now dip the washcloth into the bucket and start soaping down the top surfaces. Then rinse them with the hose sprayer. Now soap and wash down the sides of the painted surfaces only. This means no chrome has been washed yet. If you feel some grit as you wash? Stop. Squeeze out the cloth, toss it in the laundry basket, and get a new washcloth. Continue to wash until the painted surfaces are all clean and rinsed. Now wash the chrome trim, grilles, taillights, bumpers, and such. Leave the wheels for last. They will contain the most grit.

Now, some painters will use a chamois at this point to wipe and soak up all the water. I use a clean cotton towel. I feel that chamois will pick up grit, as they tend to be used for multiple wash jobs. Once I'm done washing, any clothes I used go right into the basket of laundry to be washed.

I never wax anything. Many painters will disagree with me on this point. But I have never waxed any of my bikes or cars. I use a glaze product instead. My favorite is Ultra Finish (www.ultrafinishproducts.com). Years ago one of my customers turned me onto Ultra Finish. He said it filled the slight sand scratches and made them disappear. I love the stuff. I have used it in many situations where I needed a quick remedy to a bad finish.

But I find that nearly every painter has a product that they swear by. My husband prefers Meguiar's Number 7 glaze.

And don't forget to pass on proper washing instructions to customers. A painter will save themselves a lot of headaches down the road.

HANDY HINT

Most scratch damage will happen around specific areas of the vehicle. I find these areas to be around the trunk lid keyhole, near the gas cap opening, and especially around the door handles.

CHAPTER 15
TROUBLESHOOTING

I have experienced moments in my painting career that I was not sure I would survive. What made it even worse was that in most cases the problems could have been prevented. But there is no turning back the clock and doing right whatever it was that was done wrong. This chapter deals with trying to fix the problems that do happen. These remedies are things that have worked for me . . . usually. They might be the answer to your problem. They might not. There are so many variables in custom painting that it's impossible to cover absolutely every little thing. In the past, books that that have been the most helpful to me were ones with comprehensive troubleshooting pages. In this chapter I'm doing the best I can to help when the situation seems totally bleak and hopeless.

Remember, custom painting is 60 percent common sense, 25 percent technique, and 15 percent talent. Being very patient also helps.

COLOR MATCHING FOR REPAIRS

Ah, the pure pleasure of matching your custom colors! Sooner or later, all painters find themselves in the position of having to match a custom color they painted. Maybe it's a part of the car that got damaged and the whole part needs to be painted to match. Or maybe the damage is minimal, and just a small area on the part needs repainting. Sometimes painters get inspired while applying coats of paint and throw on a little of this and a little of that and it comes out incredible. So you can't just open up a can of paint and spray away.

Hopefully, notes were kept while the color was sprayed and you still have the color sample. But notes don't always get taken and they can get lost. And the color sample was not sprayed at the same time as the parts, so there's no guarantee it's a perfect match. Plus, if it is a job that's over a year old, fading might have occurred.

Some painters are great at spot repairing candy colors. Some candy colors are easier to spot repair than others. Unless the repaired area is bordered by artwork, I usually repaint the entire candy coated area, sometimes masking off the artwork. I usually try to save the artwork. Pearl and solid colors are easier to spot repair. But if there are many layers of clear over a lot of artwork with lighter colors, you can sometimes see a shadow where the spot repair meets up with the original paint. Here's what I do when I have to match an impossible custom color. And remember, colors can also fade or change over time. So don't get discouraged

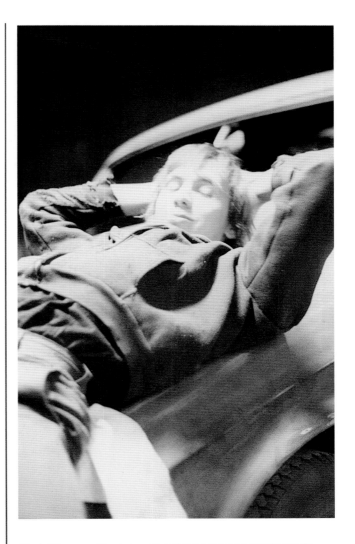

Why is this man smiling and so relaxed? He's just helping out at a friend's shop. His future in no way depends on the result of any car being worked on.

if the color matching is frustrating.

Another thing to keep in mind is that dealing with and repairing custom paint is not like dealing with factory paint. Factory paint has far less coat thickness. This means there's less chance of reactions when the coats are sanded through and the edges of each round of paint are revealed. The reactions happen when new paint reacts with the edges of the old paint. It is usually caused by the base coat, used to match the color for the repair, reacting with the sanded-through edges of the urethane used for the original paint's top coat.

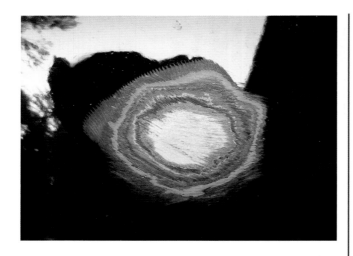
Halos.

REPAIRS

If the part is a repaired part, you've probably sanded through several rounds of urethane in feather edging the area. This will appear as "halos" in the surface around the area of the repair. The problem is that breaking through the layers can result in the layers "bleeding" up through the primer, right through the color coats.

What I do is make sure my last layer of plastic filler is a two-part flowable polyester filler putty. Then I apply a smooth, not overly thick coat of it over any place where I sanded through layers of paint. This tends to "seal" everything down. I carefully sand the filler with 180-grit paper, so my surface is as even as I can get it without going though any more layers of paint.

I mask off the repair area just beyond the plastic fill zone, maybe 2–3 inches, protecting the paint around the repair. Now I do the priming. Sometimes you're trying to save artwork, so there may not be much room. Mask off the artwork. Use your own judgment. Each situation is different.

Now spray a few coats of a two-part fill primer. Watch the area to see if anything like little cracks appear in the wet surface. This is when you'll see if there's anything going on below all those coats of paint. Sometimes the undercoats crack just beyond the dent or damage, and the color and clear coats look fine on the surface. These cracks won't be very noticeable on the sanded surface but with freshly applied paint, you will see them.

Stop painting. If there are any tiny bubbles or lifting areas, this may mean a reaction is occurring between the original paint and the repair. If there's anything but a smooth, flawless primered surface, stop painting. Let it dry, and then dig out all the area where the problem is. Using 80-grit, remove all the problem paint. Feather edge the area.

Get out the flowable filler, then fill and cover the newly sanded area. Hopefully this time all the damaged paint is gone and the repair holds. After the priming is done and dry, wet sand with 400.

COLOR MATCH

Make sure you are doing your color match on a sunny day. Start first thing in the morning. Afternoon light can have a golden glow that may affect the color match.

Go light on the coats, especially if candy paint is used. Better to go too light than too dark or too much. You can always add another coat. If the sun hides behind a cloud for the rest of the day, stop painting and check the tech sheet for the paint you are using. How long can you let the car sit without sanding if you want to recoat it? With the paint I use, I can let base coat sit 12 hours and urethane sit 3 days before recoating. Know your product. Once you've applied too much paint, it's back to square one.

One trick is to first try matching the color on a spare panel. Experiment with that and get the color perfect. Compare the color in the sun and shade. I'm such a perfectionist, I'll let paint dry dust-free on the car but still raw enough to recoat. Then, if possible, I'll roll the car outside the booth and look at it in the sun. Does it match in the sun and in the booth? Hopefully it does, your repair holds, and we all live happily ever after.

Don't lose your mind if things go wrong, like applying one too many coats of candy. Clean the guns, shut down the shop, and try again the next day. Tell your customer you'd rather have it right than wrong.

EFFECT AND CAUSE

There can many reasons for things going wrong. When things don't look right, stop painting, let it dry for a while and research the problem. The answers aren't always easy. But here are a few problems and what MAY cause them.

CRAZING OR CRACKING

If the car or parts were just removed from a colder section of the shop, and your booth or spray area is warmer, give the parts some time to heat up. Painting cold parts in a warm area, with paint that is the same temp as the area, can result in crazing or cracking. The repair can be vexing. Some painters have made saves in this area by recoating the part with overreduced paint. I have not made many saves in the crazing department. I end up sanding down the cracks, sealing them, and starting over. I don't like putting hours of artwork into base coats I have doubts with. In my early painting days I made a few trips to the sandblaster with crazed parts.

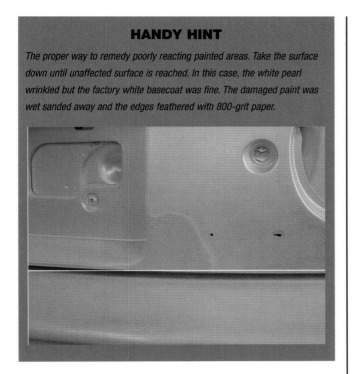

WRINKLING

Wrinkling is usually caused by trapped solvents or repenetration. When this occurs you've either used the wrong temperature range of reducer, recoated too soon, or it's way too hot to be painting. Some painters mistakenly use a cold (fast) reducer to "dry" their work quicker. Bad idea. The top dries faster and the bottom of the layer (or coat) just lies there. The drier top layer acts as a lid so it can't evaporate the solvents, and they just lie there, soaking into the layer below. If you recoat before this layer has dried, at the least you get wrinkles, and at the worst the paint will lift clear to the primer, and maybe even to the metal!

Some companies' products can be more prone to wrinkling. This is due to the "temp" of their solvents. Some paints are pretty "hot" and thoroughly penetrate the layers below. Time between coats is crucial with products like this. The window between coats is very strict. Wait a few minutes too long, it wrinkles. Lay on a coat too heavy, it wrinkles. This is especially a problem with urethane paints.

I try to use paints that are very forgiving. When I use a new product, I put it through a few tests, trying to make it wrinkle on a sample part. This is why testing your paint products is so important. A few hours testing can really save you time, money, and your sanity.

Other causes for wrinkling: bad catalyst, or uncured or soft urethane. Wrinkling can also happen when painting base coat over urethane clear that is over base coat. It begins when solvent from the top layer of base coat gets through the urethane clear in a thin or broken spot and resaturates the base coat under the clear. There'll be a layer of catalyzed clear between two wet layers of base coat.

Painting Rule Number 1 also applies in this situation. Having mishmash layers of catalyzed and uncatalyzed paint, clear, primer, and sealer is unstable. There's no telling what may happen down the road, even if it looks good. This is what happens when trying to take shortcuts. If you have any doubts, remove all the paint, right down to the substrate.

OK, what do I do if it wrinkles? Myself, I have never been able to save paint that has wrinkled. Again, I hate doing something, having it look OK, then a few days later—whammo! It's showing the wrinkled effect again, but now it's under all kinds of clear, and the customer is due to arrive shortly.

In cases where it's just a bit of wrinkling on one part, I let it dry and remove the damaged paint by wet sanding. Then I let the part dry out well, in case any of the undercoats are soft. I look very closely at them. Are there tiny wrinkles in them? If I have any doubts, I'll take it down to the metal, removing those doubts. Then I use flowable polyester filler to cover up all the layers I sanded through, because those separations between the layers might show through the base coats I'm about to reapply. Sand the filler, lay on some two-part primer. Sand, then apply epoxy primer sealer immediately, before spraying the new base coat. Make sure you give the sealer enough time to dry. The stuff I use says to wait at least 15 minutes, but no more than 12 hours. I wait a half-hour. Look very closely around the edges of the repair for tiny wrinkles after resuming paint application. If the entire part is wrinkled, sandblast and start over.

RUNS AND SAGS

Paint applied too heavy or overreduced for the conditions will cause the paint to run and sag. Maybe the wrong temp reducer was used and the paint is drying too slowly. Carefully sand the high spots. I'll wrap 600 sandpaper over Motor Guard Corporation's aluminum sanding blocks (Run Blockers) and slowly wet shave down the sag, taking care not to sand anything other than the run itself. It's too easy to get "light spots" around a run that was sanded away, especially in candy. I take down the run with the hard block, and then softly sand the whole area with a lighter grit paper, sometimes using a Motor Guard flexible pad. Beware if candy paint was run along a fender edge. Chances are you might sand through the candy, creating a light spot. What I do when that happens is leave the run alone and do my filler clear coats. This builds up the area around the run. Then it is sanded later, and there's less chance of getting into the candy coats.

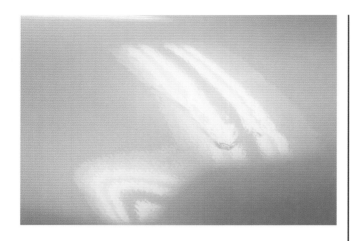

Runs and sags.

For big drips off the edges of parts, I use a new razor blade to shave off the run, and then carefully sand the edge smooth.

BUBBLES IN CLEAR

Big bubbles, lifting paint, delamination problems. These are all common problems. There are several kinds of bubbles. Some are caused by the paint lifting and not adhering to the layer below. Many are caused by some kind of solvent problems. These are usually large. The remedy? Remove the affected area. Let the paint dry and sand it off.

Figure out why the paint did not stick. In extreme cases concerning clear, it might be best to use a razor blade and literally peel the parts. Been there, done it, felt like screaming and running into the night.

SMALL BUMPY BUBBLES

Then sometimes you'll see a small bump in the paint that almost looks like dust. If it is poked at, and it flexes inward, it is a bubble. Somehow the paint did not stick in that spot. If there are a whole bunch of them, get out the 400 and take down the surface, removing all the color coats. Look carefully at the primer layer. Did the problem start there? Are there any suspicious areas or marks in the primer? If it is only one or two bubbles you may be able to save it.

Using a stencil knife, dig out the bubble. Try and see what caused it. Then wrap some 220 paper around a pen and carefully sand out the pit you dug, smoothing the edges as best you can. Sand the area around the pit with 400. Using polyester filler, dab some in there, making sure it runs over the edge. Let it dry out well. Sand and feather it without going through to the edge or disturbing the surrounding surface. You don't want deep scratches in the paint you are trying to save. Tape and paper off the area and spot prime with two-part primer. Wet sand. Now spot in the base color. After the repair is made, wet sand everything but the repair with 600. There's a good chance overspray has found its way onto the surface past the repair. Since the base

There is a bit of a problem with delamination here. I'm kidding about the "bit" part. This is actually quite serious. I used the air gun to blow this paint off. This is what happens when a painter takes shortcuts with surface preparation.

coat was cleared after the color coats were done, there is room to sand.

If you have any candy layers, I recommend respraying the candy base coat on the affected panel, unless you're a whiz at spot repairing candy. Solid and pearl colors? You should be able to spot paint the repair.

If the lifting bubbles appear all over the part? Remove all the paint. Start over.

Sometimes lifted paint bubbles that only appear over areas where bodywork was done are caused by problems with the bodywork. Usually the problem is with the hardener used with plastic filler. Maybe it's old or just bad. If this is the place you're at, get out the DA. Start over by removing all the filler. Don't try to spot repair. Problems related to sanding through all the paint layers will haunt you. So just give in, and remove all that paint and bodywork. Buy new filling material and try again. Don't use what you did before or just buy new hardener, especially if the stuff used was over a year old.

ITTY, BITTY BUBBLES

Tiny bubbles locked in the clear coat itself are usually caused by solvent drying problems. I normally run into this problem with candy and clear coats in the summer when it's hot and the humidity is high. Remedy? Stop painting. Let it dry and wet sand the affected areas. Sand away the coats containing the bubbles, then repaint. This time make sure you're using the proper temp reducer for the conditions, not waiting too long in between coats, not applying the coats too heavy, and not doing too many coats in one day. On hot, humid days, I try to be done with my candy and/or clear coat process in an hour or less.

STRANGE MARKS UNDER CLEAR COATS

Mystical fingerprints may begin appearing in the paint and under the clear weeks or months after the job is completed. No easy answer here, just hard work. Some colors can be spot repaired. But take note, sometimes rework can cause a shadow with certain light colors that have tons of clear coat on them. If a spot repair is not possible, I wet sand the affected area in the sun with 600 paper, carefully rinsing and watching as I go. What I'm doing is sanding down through my clear coats to the surface or layer that the fingerprint is on. Hopefully it's sitting on top of a clear coat, not under or in the color coats. The clear coat is where it usually happens. If it is, I sand it off, and then feather the surrounding layers of clear. Then I spot spray the area with filler clear (I use uro clear) until it is level, and then reclear the whole part. If the mark is under candy coat, start over. Do not pass Go. Do not collect $200.

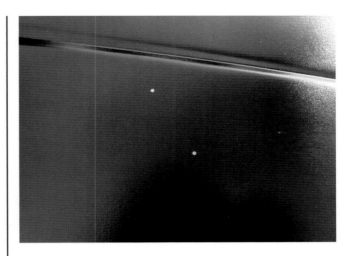

Sometimes bubbles are actually tiny water drops that got trapped under the layers of paint as it was being sprayed. Water in air lines or splashed water from watering down the booth floor will cause the paint not to stick. This shows up as little bubbles or light round spots once the "bubble" is wiped down.

HANDY HINT

Always keep current on new products. You never know when some little item will debut that may come in quite handy. For example, there are times when very small chips happen as a vehicle is coming together. Then I have to take my little paint brush and try and touch it up. These two goodies from E-Z Mix Company are designed especially for this problem. The E-Z Dabber works great for those excruciating microscopic chips. The Touch-N-Go Precision Applicator is pretty neat. Use the syringe to pull up the paint, attach the tip, and the paint flows through the tip into the repair area. I have had many projects where these would have come in handy.

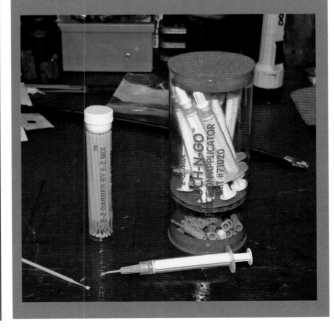

Black paint has dripped onto this flamed surface.

PULLING UP TAPE AND PAINT COMES WITH IT

Say a prayer that this is only happening in this one spot. Look at the edges of the spot. Use a stencil knife to poke the broken edge and see if the whole layer is lifting. Hopefully you did everything correctly, thoroughly sanded all the coats that needed to be sanded, and used the proper grit paper. If so, then this may just be an isolated incident. Featheredge the area. If it's quite deep, fill the pit with polyester filler, tape it off, spot prime, spot paint, and rework the artwork. If shortcuts were taken, you're not 100 percent sure of the adhesion of the paint layers, or if someone else did the base coats, there's a serious problem. Stick 2-inch tape onto the part, let it sit a while, then rip off the tape. In short, test the part to see if it keeps happening. If it does, remove all the paint.

DRIPPED OR SPILLED PAINT ON A FRESHLY AIRBRUSHED SURFACE

Let it dry. Hopefully there are lots of clear coat layers protecting the base coat color. Damp sand off any paint on the unairbrushed surface and rework any artwork. Don't worry if an outline of the drip can still be seen. After you clear coat, just retouch that area again with the airbrush and it will be completely perfect.

If the drip or spill is on the clear, just let it dry and wet sand it off. Sometimes it can be quickly wiped off.

WHAT YOU SHOULD NEVER DO

Never, never, never bake paint in the sun. I tried it once. Extremely bad idea. Evil bubbles appeared, and my Number 1 Painting Rule applied. I don't know why it happened, although I'm sure someone could explain it to me. That was eight years ago, and now I never let paint that's less than four days old sit in the sun for any length of time. As a rule, I do not bake parts that have artwork. Not even in a professional bake booth.

AIRBRUSH PROBLEMS

It depends on the airbrush being used. But keeping the airbrush very clean is the best way to keep it working fine. At the start of each airbrush session, I remove the needle and give it a quick wipe with thinner. Here are just a few problems and their causes and remedies.

Paint spitting out of airbrush, very grainy, and doesn't have an even, smooth flow

Cause: Paint is too thick.
Remedy: Thin down paint and/or raise air pressure.

Paint comes out of airbrush even when the trigger is not pulled back

Cause 1: Something—maybe dried paint, a hair, a fiber, whatever—is caught in the tip, causing the needle not to close into the tip properly.

Cause 2: Wear and tear on needle and/or on tip is causing paint to escape through those gaps.

It could also be caused by paint leaking into the air passages, as described in the next column.
Remedy 1: Remove needle and tip and clean both thoroughly. Very carefully, use an old airbrush needle to poke into tip and see if there's anything caught in the passage.
Remedy 2: Replace worn parts. Replace needle first. If problem is still present, replace tip.

Some tips are held in place by threads, and the little wrench that comes with the airbrush must be used to unscrew the tip. Other tips are simply pushed in place and held there by friction. Take care with those, as they can fall out very easily when you're working on the airbrush. Work over a towel. That way the tip won't roll away and be lost forever.

No paint comes out of airbrush, or trigger must be pulled back farther than normal to get paint flow

Cause: Something is caught in paint passages.
Remedy: Remove needle and tip, and clean them and the paint passages in airbrush body thoroughly.

Air flow is not consistent

Cause: Spray regulator or airbrush head is not sealing properly, causing outside air to affect airflow. It could be loose or, with some airbrushes, the head washer could be worn.
Remedy: Remove spray regulator or head. Look to see if sealing surfaces are clean and free of debris. Replace head washer if applicable.

No paint comes out when using bottle-feed airbrush

Cause: Either the tube or siphon cap is clogged, or the air hole in top of the cap is clogged.
Remedy: Check and clean paint passage up from bottle and clear out air hole.

Needle does not move smoothly when pulled back

Cause: Paint may have leaked back past the needle seal and is sticking in the "machinery" that pulls the needle back.
Remedy: Remove needle and chuck and spring assembly. Take assembly apart and thoroughly clean. Remove trigger. Clean out airbrush inner body with cotton swabs. Use small, round brush to clean out needle chucking guide. Reassemble. If paint has been leaking into these areas, the seal or packing that seals the head from the body is worn. In some airbrushes, it is not too hard to replace. In others, it is a total pain. I usually buy a new airbrush or try not to let very reduced paint sit in the airbrush. Very reduced paint will leak out faster than thick paint. Paint leaking into the airbrush body can also leak into the air passages. Clean out the body and if possible take apart air inlet and clean. Remove head assembly, reinstall trigger, and blow air through the brush until it comes out clean.

Use common sense when troubleshooting airbrush problems. Stay calm and investigate the problem, thinking it through. And always protect the business end of the airbrush. Keep protective caps in place when brushes are not being used.

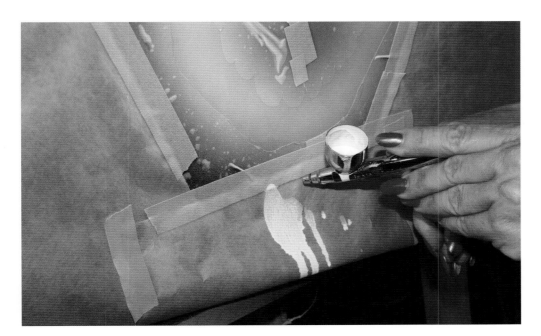

This is what happens when the cap is not tightened downs securely on a gravity feed airbrush cup, and the reason why a painter should always thoroughly mask off around the artwork area. While this spill would be relatively easy to damp sand away if spilled on a urethane base, if it was spilled on basecoat, it may have been a disaster.

INDEX

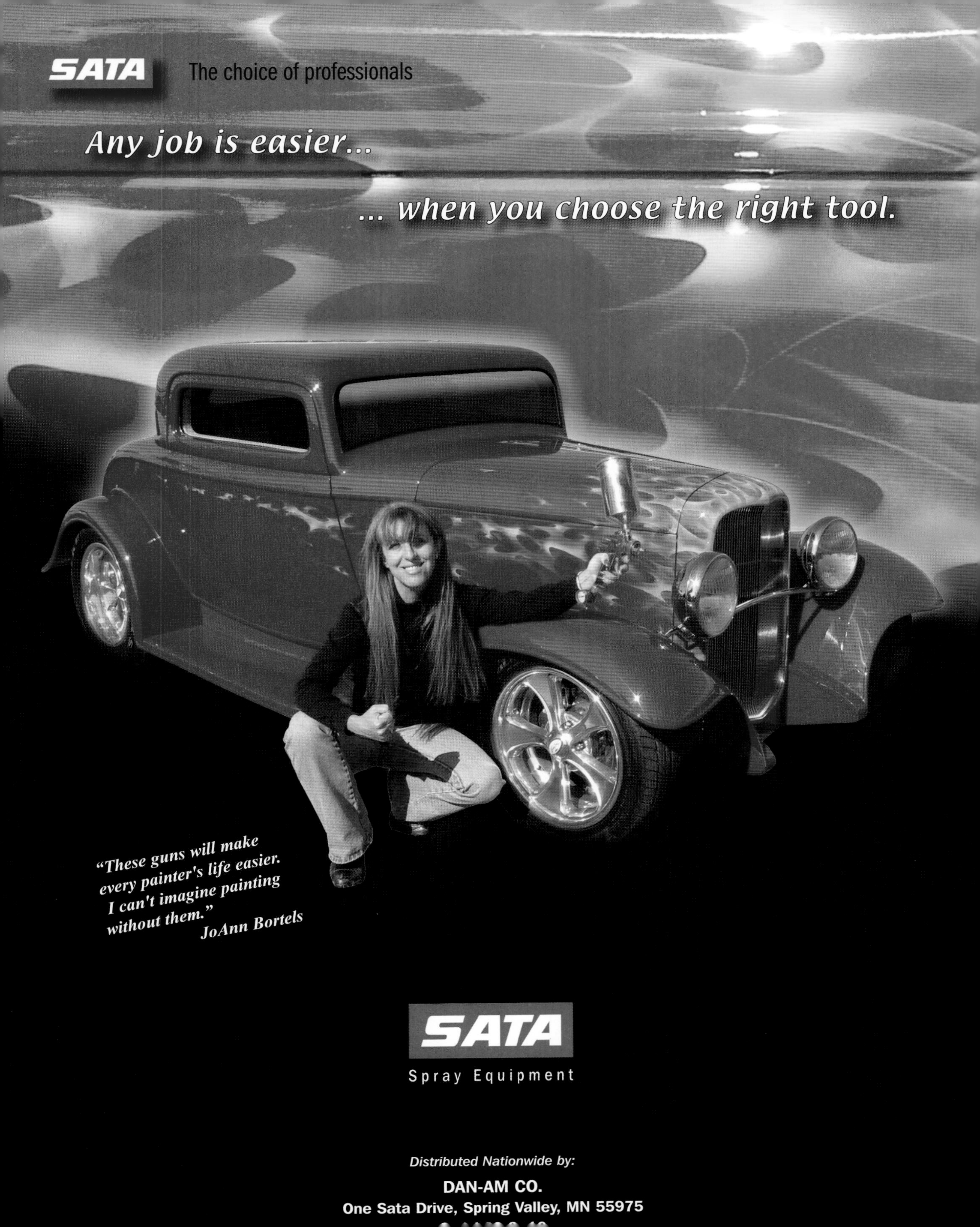
SATA
The choice of professionals
Any job is easier...
... when you choose the right tool.
"These guns will make every painter's life easier. I can't imagine painting without them."
JoAnn Bortels
SATA
Spray Equipment
Distributed Nationwide by:
DAN-AM CO.
One Sata Drive, Spring Valley, MN 55975

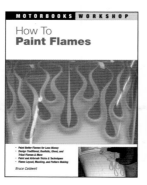

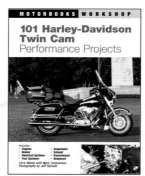
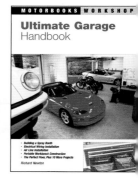